39-23

THE BEGINNING KINDERGARTEN TEACHER

by

LORRAINE SALOT
Kindergarten Teacher
Detroit Public Schools

and

JEROME E. LEAVITT
Professor of Education
University of Arizona

Burgess Publishing Company

426 South Sixth Street • Minneapolis, Minnesota 55415

Burgess

EDUCATION SERIES

Consulting Editor — Laurence S. Flaun

3 /27/74 Baker & Tyly 3. 95

Preface

Teaching five year olds can be a most satisfying experience, and the beginning kindergarten teacher has many happy teaching days to which to look forward. The informality of the program, the close teacher-pupil relationships which evolve, the tremendous rate of growth of children during this year, and the unexpected learning experiences which arise, all tend to make this a unique experience.

Not every kindergarten teacher will find himself in an ideal situation, with a spacious, light, airy room, equipped with adequate toys and materials, adjacent to a well protected outdoor play area, and with a small class of children; but whatever the situation, the teacher faces a challenge to give his pupils the most that is possible during the year they spend with him. This guide has been prepared as a resource book to assist the kindergarten teacher to provide these rich experiences for boys and girls.

It was not the intention of the writers to make this a theory book, but rather provide practical suggestions which can be used in most kindergartens.

There are always many ways of doing things, some just as good as others, and those mentioned here should not be considered the only ways; but they are offered with the idea that they will be helpful to the beginning kindergarten teacher when he is first starting out, or to the experienced teacher as he searches for better ways of working with boys and girls.

It is our hope that the suggestions given in this volume will help to prevent problems which otherwise might arise. May it help the teacher to make his teaching effective and satisfying in this delightful field of work, kindergarten teaching.

Lorraine Salot
Jerome E. Leavitt

Table of Contents

Chapter I

The Child and Kindergarten

There are a great many people who think of kindergarten merely as a place where children play all the time and learn to get along with others. This is important, indeed, but actually, much more than this is going on in a good kindergarten. The kindergarten program is set up to meet the present needs of five year olds, and to provide them with the background of experiences they will need for later ventures into reading, arithmetic, science, social studies, music, art, literature, in fact, every field of learning.

One would not expect to find a child in kindergarten doing a complicated problem in mathematics, yet the foundation for mathematics is started in the pre-school and kindergarten years through simple experiences with numbers. College subjects have their beginnings there. Discovering what a magnet can do is the child's introduction to physics. Realizing that steam and ice are other forms of water is the beginning of an important concept in chemistry. There is no other grade which includes so much in its content, for the content of the kindergarten includes every area of subject matter, but on a level that the five year old can understand.

Because of the informality of a good kindergarten program and its freedom from a rigid time schedule, it is possible to give the child a number of first hand experiences where he can learn by doing, provide time for him to experiment and discover things for himself, and provide an opportunity for him to follow up on his particular interests and those of the group. All of this results in learning that is meaningful and which is retained for a long period of time.

The final goal is not merely the accumulation of knowledge, but the developmental growth of the whole child, physically, socially, emotionally, intellectually and spiritually. The atmosphere of the kindergarten plays an important part in whether or not these goals are attained. In this day and age, when our concerns are so great about the mental health of the population, we are beginning to realize the importance of the early emotional climate in a child's life. We have learned that many disorders in later life stem from emotional crises which occurred in childhood. Teachers in general are in a good position to see when crises arise, but kindergarten teachers especially have the opportunity of creating a healthy atmosphere, not one where children do entirely as they please, nor one where children do only what pleases the teacher, but rather an atmosphere of acceptance, friendliness, and one conducive to growth and learning, where the teacher guides and helps each individual grow physically, socially, emotionally, intellectually and spiritually. Kindergarten involves much more than play, as an examination of a good program will reveal.

The Kindergarten Program

Much of the kindergarten program can be seasonal in nature, that is, dealing with changes that take place in fall, winter, spring, or summer, or concerned with special days, such as Halloween or Christmas, for these are important in the child's world. But the five year old is also interested in many other things, some of interest for only ten or fifteen minutes, and some for days or weeks. The teacher must constantly evaluate and decide what interests of the group will provide the most worthwhile learning experiences. As many interest areas fall into a given month, the kindergarten teacher might find it helpful to consider the possible activities throughout the entire year. The asterisks in the list that follows designate activities that do not specifically relate to the month under which they are listed but have been put there because of tradition and balance of program.

September
* Safety
* Homes
* Families
  Beginnings of Fall
* Fruits and vegetables
  Preparation for Winter (animals, people)

October
  Fall continued
  Halloween (safety emphasized)
  Fire Prevention Week

November
  Further observation of Fall and preparation for Winter
  Thanksgiving, including history simply told
* Sources of foods
* Farms
  Veterans' Day (simple patriotic ideas)

December
  Christmas and Hanukkah
  Beginnings of Winter

January
  Winter (in nature, sports, the child's life)
  Feeding birds

February
  Valentines
  Simple patriotic ideas

March
  Wind
* Beginnings of Spring

April
  Spring
  Easter

May
    Mothers' Day
    Gardens
    Flowers
  * Birds
    Butterflies
    Insects

June
    Fathers' Day
    Vacations
    Summer sports
    Summer safety (traffic, boating, swimming)
    Seashore collections

Areas of interest which might fall into any month include: Safety, Homes, Families, Fruits, Vegetables, Other Foods, Farms, Birds, Birthdays, Stories, Transportation, Pets, Modern Inventions, Indians, Community Helpers, Circus, Health, Safety, Space Ideas, Television Programs, Science.

In order to provide the proper activities and experiences for his particular group, the teacher must know the characteristics of typical five year olds, those of his particular class, the needs of each one as an individual, and then plan accordingly.

Characteristics of Five Year Olds

As no two children are alike, not every child, of course, will be as pictured below. Briefly, however, on the basis of mental, language, social, emotional, and physical characteristics, the five year old may be described in this way:

Mental characteristics. He is curious about many things, is interested in everything in his world, such as animals, people, plants, and machines. He learns chiefly by experience and observation. His attention span is short, at first, but increases during the year. He is interested in numbers, how many things there are, and can count to about ten. He has only a limited concept of time and space. He is able to distinguish between truth and fantasy, but his imagination is vivid.

Language characteristics. He uses speech well in conversation, and it is quite clear, free from infantile articulation. He is able to make all of the speech sounds but has not mastered them, that is, to the point where he uses them correctly and consistently. F, v, zh, sh, l, th as in that, and th as in think, s, z, and r have not been mastered. (See Mastery Chart on page 7) He can tell the plot of a story, and has a vocabulary of about 2,200 words. His questions are now more relevant and meaningful, and often direct and personal.

Social characteristics. His language ability affects his social adjustment. He seeks friendships, yet sometimes likes to play alone. He is willing to share and has developed a sense of ownership. He is eager to please, is serious, and quite purposeful. When thwarted, he is likely to sulk, or destroy a possession of one who has caused the thwarting. He is amused by noises, funny faces, and things falling upside down.

<u>Emotional characteristics</u>. He is quite stable emotionally, and usually dependable, obedient, and cooperative, but sometimes impulsive. His desire for attention leads to showing off by performing stunts or calling out. He is eager to work and anxious to attain a feeling of accomplishment. He craves recognition and praise. He may show jealousy of others because of their prestige in games or friendships.

<u>Physical characteristics</u>. He is very active physically and able to skip, jump, dance, and control his body well. He is fatigued by inactivity, and becomes restless. He shows greater command of the use of tools than before, such as brushing teeth, combing hair, but has some difficulty using small muscles, for the accessory muscles which control fingers are not completely developed at this stage. Right or left handedness has developed, and about ninety per cent are right handed. His eyes are not mature, and there is a tendency toward far-sightedness. Eye-hand coordination is difficult for him. His ability to hear is well developed. Masturbation is common, but does not have a connotation of wrong. He is highly susceptible to disease at this age.

Needs of a Five Year Old and How Kindergarten Tries to Meet Them

What does this child need at five years of age, and can it be provided for him? The teacher must be aware of these needs for the entire kindergarten program and its philosophy is built around them.

INTELLECTUAL NEEDS
>To have experiences to satisfy his curiosity.
>To be given guidance to help him succeed.
>To have successful enterprises and the enjoyment of a feeling of accomplishment.
>To receive clarification of ideas.
>To be allowed time to solve problems.

<u>We try to meet them by:</u>
>Providing opportunities to observe, to experiment, and to learn through doing.
>Helping each child according to his ability, so that each may reach his greatest potentiality, and be challenged in so doing.
>Keeping activities simple, and not judging children's work by adult standards.
>Taking time to straighten out misconceptions, to explain meanings of new words.
>Encouraging children to figure out things for themselves, in work, play and games, yet helping them over the difficult spots through stimulating questioning and explanation.
>Providing many stories, visual aids, and other learning devices.

LANGUAGE NEEDS
>To have freedom to express himself.
>To enjoy communication.

To hear correct speech.
To be free from tension.
To have opportunities to use sounds and speech.
To have opportunities for listening.

We try to meet them by:
Providing opportunities for conversation in small, informal groups (as in play, work and games) as well as in the large class group. The teacher articulating properly, and pronouncing correctly words which the children mispronounce, without making an issue of it nor interrupting.
Developing awareness of words which sound alike.
Maintaining a pleasant, relaxed atmosphere, where the children feel comfortable.
Providing listening activities, such as story time, news time, and discussion periods.

SOCIAL NEEDS
To live in an atmosphere of friendliness and affection.
To become independent and self directive.
To become cooperative in group participation.
To become aware of responsibilities to others.
To share in making decisions.
To develop habits of courtesy and to respect authority.

We try to meet them by:
Becoming acquainted with each child as an individual, and developing pleasant teacher-child relationships.
Letting the child do as many things for himself as he is capable of doing.
Encouraging the child, when he is ready, to enter into group activities, such as rhythms, games, and plays.
Providing many opportunities for sharing (as in getting materials, playing games, doing special "jobs").
Directing his aggressiveness from undesirable to desirable behavior.
Providing opportunities for discussions of problems which arise, and for participation in developing rules of conduct.
Encouraging him to say, "please", "thank you", "pardon me", and other acts of courtesy, and to realize his responsibility toward others.

EMOTIONAL NEEDS
To express himself.
To experience the joy of creating.
To find release from tension.
To learn self-control in order that he may enjoy working with others.
To be loved and to give love.
To direct his energies properly toward desirable action.
To feel he "belongs".

We try to meet them by:
Providing opportunity to communicate his ideas and feelings in some art form, such as paint, crayons, clay, colored paper, music or rhythms.

Encouraging original ideas and creativity, not only in work but in play by creating games, stories, songs, and poems.

Providing activities which allow freedom to move about and talk freely (as in work and play) and to express his feelings in art, music, and dramatic play.

Helping the child develop proper attitudes toward others, and especially toward himself, and to develop other good habits of mental health. Helping him learn to follow directions and become a responsible member of the group.

Providing activities in which each individual is skilled or can be the center of interest.

Giving deserved praise and recognition often.

PHYSICAL NEEDS

To have vigorous activity - a chance to run, jump, climb, balance.

To change body position often, because of stress in striated muscles.

To rest after activity.

To have the proper amount of sleep and food for his body.

To develop good health and dental habits.

To engage in large muscle activity.

To develop good safety habits.

We try to meet them by:

Providing frequent outdoor play periods, rhythmic activities, games, (indoors and out) and activities which involve different parts of the body.

Not expecting children to sit for too long a period at a time.

Alternating between active and quiet activities.

Encouraging children to use the lavatory properly, and to wash hands after going to the toilet and before eating, to cover the mouth when sneezing or coughing.

Teaching the importance of proper care of the teeth.

Providing large crayons, picture books, paint and crayon paper in order to emphasize large muscle, rather than small muscle activities.

Developing the proper care in crossing streets.

Speech of the Kindergarten Child

Language plays such an important role in the life of everyone, that it is important for teachers to understand the development of speech in the child, some defects that might appear, and what they, as teachers, might do to improve speech in the classroom.

Development of speech. The first words used by babies begin with m, w, p, b, t, d, or n sounds, and are repetitive. In English, French, German, Spanish, Swedish, Greek, and Russian, "mama" is one of the words for mother, so when the child utters this sound, we think he is saying a word meaning mother. Beginning with these first sounds of words, until about age three, the child is in the speech readiness period, first using name words, then short, simple sentences, then longer ones, until by age three he is usually using speech very well in conversation. Not all sounds are completely mastered by this age, that is, mastered to the point where they are used correctly and consistently as is shown below.

MASTERY CHART [1]

Age in years	Sounds
$3\frac{1}{2}$	p b m w h
$4\frac{1}{2}$	d t n g k ng y j
$5\frac{1}{2}$	f
$6\frac{1}{2}$	v zh sh l th (as in that)
$7\frac{1}{2}$	s z r wh th (as in think)

When the child enters kindergarten at four and a half or five, he may be able to make all of these sounds, but at this age, he has not yet mastered them completely. So much maturation takes place during this year, that the ordinary kindergarten program helps the child to develop rapidly in his speech and to overcome many speech difficulties he might have. At first, the children will all want to talk at once, but when standards have been set up for taking turns in group discussion, and for listening politely, group conversations become worthwhile language - learning situations, as plans are made for the day, experiences are shared, handwork is discussed, or stories told. Even more important to the child's language development are the opportunities for the child to talk freely with others, during work, play, game time, and science activities, to say nothing of the valuable contribution to speech development that is made during dramatic play, radio and television shows put on by children, dramatizations, puppet shows, and the music period, with its singing, dancing, pretending things to music, playing instruments and other rhythm work.

Improvement of speech in kindergarten. If the kindergarten teacher is to do his part in speech correction, he needs a systematic means of discovering which children have speech deficiencies. A collection of pictures or real objects, the name or color of which contains a specific speech sound, can be used as such a test. The following objects or pictures are possibilities:

baby	glass	moon	soup	wolf
cat	jacket	nose	sugar	yellow
dog	key	pencil	toy	zebra
face	light	rope	valentine	chair

[1] Poole, I. "Genetic Development of Articulation of Consonant Sounds in Speech." Elementary English Review, II (1934) p. 159-161.

With the help of such a test, and the ordinary communication which takes place between child and teacher, speech defects noted might be classified as follows:

Classification	Symptoms
Stutter	Blocking, unable to talk or to get started. Repetition of sounds (c-c-cat). An appearance of negativism, which may indicate a silent stutterer.
Oral inactivity	Substitutions of sounds, "wabbit" for "rabbit." Omission of sounds, "how" for "house". Distortion of sounds "shoup" for "soup". Addition of sounds, "buhlue" for "blue".
Lisp	"Th" substituted for sibilants. Sound coming over the sides of the tongue, as in a lateral lisp.
(Less common ones) Cleft palate Cerebral Palsy Hard of Hearing Speech Disorders of Voice	Voice that is hoarse, husky, weak, nasal, or monotonous.
Baby Talk (Not a true speech defect) Foreign Accent (Not a true speech defect)	

The classifications above are those used by the Speech Correction Department in the Detroit Public Schools and are similar to those used by other school systems. In schools where there is a speech teacher he will want the names of all who seem to have speech defects, and, if the case is severe enough, might include the child in his speech classes. The kindergarten teacher himself, however, can help those who have oral inactivity right in the classroom, with all children taking part through specific activities such as;

In rhythms:
    For "r" sound: Pretending they are bears or lions, growling "rrr"
    For "j" sound: Pretending they are frogs, saying "jee-jooms".
    For "z" sound: Pretending they are bees flying, and buzzing "zzz"
    For "ch" sound: Pretending they are trains, saying, "choo-choo".

For "k" sound: Pretending they are crows, saying "kuh-kuh-kuh".

For "g" sound: Pretending they are trains, saying "chug-chug-chug".

In singing:

For "m" sound: Humming tunes of songs.

For "l" sound: Singing "la-la-la" instead of the words of a song.

For breath
control: Whistling tunes.

For "t" sound: (To the tune of Oats, Peas, Beans, and Barley Grow)
I found a toy on the Christmas tree. And this is the way it played for me. Toot toot toot - toot toot - toot toot
And this is the way it played for me.

In games involving speech, and sounds, singing.

In literature, dramatizations, shadow plays, puppet shows, by children.

It is just as important for the teacher to know the things he must not do nor say, as to know techniques for helping speech. Speech therapists suggest the following DON'TS:

Don't correct a child while he is talking, nor interrupt him in the middle of a sentence.

Don't discuss his speech where he can hear you.

Don't rush him when he has something to say.

If he stutters, don't try to help him along by supplying the word, asking him to "start over", nor saying "Take your time." Wait patiently.

Don't emphasize a certain sound, such as "rrrun", or "lllamp". It is unnatural. Let him say it as best he can.

DO, however, be a good example yourself, using clear, un-hurried proper speech.

Chapter II

Preparation for the First Day

When the beginning teacher starts his first teaching assignment, he will be on his own for the first time, as there will not be a supervising teacher at his side to help him out of difficulties, guide his teaching, nor answer his questions. There will be many people and things new to him: the administration, the school itself, and the community. The beginning teacher will find it helpful to have some knowledge of these before his first day with the pupils. In addition it will be important to have his room arranged properly, to have the appropriate toys and materials on hand, to have definite plans made for registration and to have complete plans worked out for the first day.

Orientation of the Teacher

In some school systems there is a definite period set aside before classes start, for teachers to become acquainted with important phases of the school system. Other school systems help teachers by means of handbooks made available to each one.

The size of the school and the type of the community have a lot to do with the ease with which the new teacher adapts himself to his first school. The following information may be helpful in becoming oriented to a new situation.

The administration. Whereas his contact with a principal might have been limited during his student teaching days, as a teacher he will be responsible to the principal for everything he does, and therefore will want to understand and respect the principal's authority. The principal is the head of the school. In some schools there is also an assistant principal, who, under the general direction of the principal, assists with supervision of teachers, non-instructional personnel, the children, and acts for the principal in his absence. However, the principal is in complete charge of everything in his building. A modern administrator is not a dictator, for he realizes the importance of running his school democratically, keeping parents, children, and teachers well informed and providing proper supervision of the instructional program. He is responsible to the superintendent for the welfare of the pupils. As the principal delegates this responsibility to the teachers, the beginning teacher needs to appreciate how great it is, and in order to avoid making serious mistakes, should become acquainted, as early as possible, with important legal and safety regulations, usually listed in the local Board of Education handbook or guide. Some important items that are included in a number of these handbooks are listed below:

No child may stand on a chair.
Children must not be left in a room without a teacher.

Decorations must be fireproof.

No candles may be lit, nor fire of any kind created.

All students must be dismissed at the regular time.

Requests for early dismissal or dismissal to person other than
parent must be approved by the office.

In spite of everything, accidents do occur. If they do, the principal's office should be notified immediately, and if necessary, an accident report prepared. Whether the teacher has been negligent, or not, it will be to his advantage to have notified the principal in case of any repercussions.

Each principal has his own way of helping the beginning teacher. Some appoint an experienced teacher to act as advisor, while others hold orientation meetings for all newcomers. The present trend seems to be toward principal-teacher conferences as an orientation procedure.

The beginning teacher who develops a good working relationship with his principal and other staff members will find greater satisfaction in his work. Such a teacher will not run to the principal with every petty problem which arises, nor will he monopolize teachers' meetings with his personal problems or opinions. He will seek help when it is necessary and invite the principal to see first hand, the problem situation, if there is one and will keep the principal informed of any unusual developments or problems.

The school building and community. As early as possible, the new teacher should acquaint himself with the school community and the school building. A drive through the streets of the school district will help him understand the area with which his kindergarten children are familiar, their homes, play facilities, and general socio-economic and cultural background. A walk around the block will reveal many ideas for "trips" later on in the term. A fire hydrant, fire alarm box, mail box, garden, bushes, trees, squirrel's nest, bird's nest, telephone pole, traffic light, though common, are not understood by all children. They are easily visited and have many learning possibilities.

The new teacher will want to become familiar with what audio-visual equipment is available and if he does not already know how will want to learn to use it sometime during the first few weeks. He also will also find it helpful to become acquainted with the library, science room and other special rooms for he will have many reasons for using these facilities later on.

Kindergarten classes. Although the principal is responsible for the assignment of students to specific class sections, teachers are usually consulted regarding these assignments. The grouping of children on the basis of those who will work well together and with a specific teacher is receiving favor in many schools.

Most kindergartens admit children in September only, and keep them for a year, while a few others begin a second semester in February. In the latter case, it is helpful to both teacher and child to combine the beginners with those starting the second term. The second term children enjoy helping the teacher show the new children about the room, how to get materials, put them back, and the many other routine procedures which need to be learned. The child who during the first term was timid and retiring feels important in his new role as "teacher", and gains confidence when chosen to "take care of" a new child.

It is true that those who have already had one term of kindergarten ought to be capable of more than those just starting, but very often an advanced beginner is far more mature than an immature second term child. The good teacher keeps the individual child in mind, does not expect more than he is capable of, and helps each one to achieve his maximal potentiality.

If the groups are combined, the child in the second term will not be repeating his first term, just because he is with beginners. The entire kindergarten program throughout the year follows the seasons, is based on the philosophy of following up the worthwhile things that are of interest to children, and to fulfilling the needs of the individual.

Arrangement of the Room

In preparing for the first day of kindergarten, some thought should be given to the arrangement of the room. Often the kindergarten teacher is placed in a situation where he shares a room with others. If this is the case it is necessary to arrive at an arrangement of the room that satisfies both teachers. Regardless of who is responsible for the room arrangement, certain specific items need to be considered in relationship to the activities included in the curriculum.

Blocks. Blocks should be stored close to an open area where they are to be used, and arranged so that children may take them out and put them back easily by themselves. (The ideal spot would be in an alcove, where finished construction could be left standing as long as the interest lasts, and not be torn down every day only to be rebuilt the next day.)

Toys. Toys should be spaced around the room so that children will not have to crowd around the same shelf in order to get a toy. All of the same kind should be together, if at all possible, that is, all puzzles together, all matching games together, and so forth. "A place for everything and everything in its place" is a good motto. However, the place should be a logical one, easy for the children to use, easy to remember, or indicated by a picture, and not changed unless everyone is told about the change.

Doll corner. The doll corner may be expanded and contracted as necessary, if the doll table is placed on the outskirts of the corner, where it can be moved in or out at will.

Store. A permanent store may be built of blocks along a short space of wall near tables, and the tables arranged in an "L" shape for a counter. The teacher might keep this in mind and early in the term help the children work it out in this way.

Sand table. The sand table should be in an out of the way place, so that spilled sand will not be a hazard in an activity area.

Piano. The piano may be used as a divider or partition, for a doll corner, book nook, or to hide blocks, but arranged in such a way that there is never any danger of it falling over. If not protected by shelves, it is best never to allow children behind the piano.

Library corner. A book case or a shelf of books for children's use should be located in a well lighted area of the room, preferably near the windows, and close to tables where they are to be used.

Science table. A science table or display area should be ready for possible collections, or items of interest as they are brought in by teacher or children.

Numerals display. Numerals from 0 to 10, with the appropriate number of items for each numeral, might be a permanent display on a bulletin board to be used throughout the year for providing counting experiences.

Open area. A large open area should be available near the piano for games, rhythms, and singing. This should be so located that children will not face the light when sitting in a group, as it is hard on their eyes. Space should be adequate to prevent crowding children into a small area where they are uncomfortable and too close to each other for normal changes of position. Many behavior problems can be avoided simply by providing adequate space between children.

Paint table. The paint table should be located near the cupboard where the paints are kept, in order that they need not be carried any greater distance than necessary. Easels should be located so that children will not bump into them.

Display boards. The room should be as attractive as possible. Have colorful and interesting display boards ready the first day. It is important to display children's work, but until this is available, the teacher should arrange one or two displays on a familiar subject such as nursery rhymes, favorite stories, children "doing things", pets, or animals, including one involving numbers for experience in counting. To be effective, a display board need not be a work of art, nor need it involve many hours of work. A simple, attractive one, which makes children think, is all that is necessary. Such a display can usually be made by selecting pictures from your picture collection or securing a loan exhibit from the library. Third dimensional effects make display boards more fun.

A growing picture collection is one of the tools of a good teacher.

Appropriate Toys and Materials

Because beginning kindergarten children are likely to get puzzles mixed up, and lose some of the parts, it is wise to have only two or three simple puzzles available at first, until they are taught the proper care of them, to put them back only after they are finished. The teacher might suggest that if a child cannot do a puzzle himself, he ask someone to do it with him. If the two of them cannot finish it together, they should ask the teacher to help. In this way they will soon learn to complete all puzzles before putting them away and gradually more and more can be made available.

At the beginning of the term, only a few lotto games should be available, but gradually more games may be included as they learn not to mix up the parts of the games.

Scissors can be dangerous if not carried properly, and a mischievous newcomer just might decide to cut someone's hair if scissors are out the first day. It is better not to put them out until there is time for proper instruction for using and carrying them.

Choice toys or materials should be put away also, until the teacher knows his group and has time for discussion about their care.

If the teacher plans to have children use crayons the first day, he will want an adequate supply of paper available, plus a reserve supply ready in case of emergency.

Registration Day

In the light of our present knowledge of little children and the impact which the first day of school has upon them, it is important that time be provided for meeting the children on registration day, and conferring with their parents. If half hour appointments are made, ten such conference periods can be handled in a day, or fifty in one week. The advantage of such a procedure would far outweigh the disadvantages of missing a number of school days. Pre-registration programs have been a step in the right direction. In this manner many schools provide the child and his parents with a fine opportunity to become acquainted with the teacher, the room, and the school in general.

In some large schools, however, pre-registration day means only that it takes place a little earlier. The teacher has little chance to confer with the parent, nor to say more than "Hello" to the child, when there are fifty other parents waiting in line to be taken care of. In such situations, the following suggestions may be helpful.

Name tags. Shirt cardboards or tagboard, cut into pieces about $2\frac{1}{2}$ by 4 make fine name tags. As the child is registered, the teacher can print the child's name with a felt pen or crayon, and give it to his mother to pin on him with a large safety pin, or hang around his neck on a ribbon, for the first day of kindergarten. If the first name is printed large, it can be easily read at a distance. The last name and room number might be smaller.

Emergency telephone numbers. Often an emergency arises, sometimes even on the first day of kindergarten, and parents cannot be reached at their telephone number. In such a situation, an emergency telephone number is very valuable. Telephone directories should be available for reference. Registration information should include both name and "at work" phone numbers and possibly an additional person who may be called in emergencies when parents cannot be reached.

Good Parent-school Relationships. Registration day provides the first opportunity for good parent-school relationships. At the present time, when parents are urged to visit and learn more about their schools, and are so eager to do so, the role of the teacher in public relations is a most important one. A parent forms his first impression of the school from the kindergarten teacher who registers his child. The impression he carries home should be a favorable one. A pleasant, courteous, professional attitude on the part of the teacher, and a warm, honest, mature manner can initiate a friendly, cooperative relationship. A sincere note of welcome, giving school hours, procedures, and other helpful information will be appreciated by most parents. Such a note should also include requests that parents put names in children's boots and other clothes, loops in coats or jackets so they may be hung up more easily, or any other ideas the teacher might want to convey. To be sure that they reflect school policy these notes should be approved by the school principal.

Advice on Record Keeping

When registration is over, records need to be prepared for each child. If there is not enough time to complete them all before the children come for the first time, certain ones, at least, should be ready in order to make it easier to take attendance and to report correct enrollment to the office.

A list of children, with boys and girls listed separately can be prepared in ink, but with the children numbered in pencil. As changes occur, when children transfer to or from other schools, the pencil number can be erased and the list renumbered. Whatever forms are used for recording children's absences should be prepared with at least the children's names, before they arrive for the first time. Attendance can then be taken quickly, and additional information required may be added at a later date.

Care should be taken in preparing records so that the writing and printing is legible and neatly done for many of the records will be in use during the child's entire school life.

Chapter III

The First Day of Kindergarten

With the necessary records ready, the room arranged attractively and ready for activities, with definite plans made for the day, the teacher should be well prepared to provide a happy experience for each child on his first day in kindergarten.

The first day is a most important one to all concerned, the child, the teacher, and the parent. It is important to the child for he is starting something new and significant. It is important to the teacher because he wants it to be a happy, successful beginning. It is important to the mother for varying reasons. For some mothers, this may be a difficult day, for it is hard for her to give up her baby and realize the child is growing up. For another, it might be a welcome relief to be away from the child for part of the day. For still another, it is a happy occasion, for she realizes the great adventure the child is starting, and having sensibly prepared both the child and herself for it, is able to share his joy in starting a new phase of his life.

Most children enter happily into the kindergarten atmosphere as they wave a "goodbye" to mother. Some need a few words of reassurance that mother will be back for them. A few, and fortunately, it is only a few, are not quite able to make the break away from mother, and tears roll down their cheeks.

What to Do About the Child Who Won't Leave His Mother

If classes are small, the solution may be to invite the mother to stay for a while. However, if one is invited, others will want to stay, and unless the room is of adequate size, this makes it difficult for all. The teacher must be very tactful in handling such situations, and should assure parents that they will be most welcome to visit later on.

Rather than force the reluctant child to stay and tear him from his mother, thereby making school a frightening experience for him, the teacher might explain to the mother that with so many other new children, it is difficult to give him the individual attention he needs on that day, when he has so many other new children to take care of. The teacher might then suggest that the mother keep the child at home for four or five days, until the teacher has had a chance to help the others feel secure. By that time, the teacher will be free to give the individual attention he may need. The teacher might express a sincere wish to the child to see him again some other day, and to have him in kindergarten, when he is feeling better.

Sometimes a mother will urge the teacher to let the child stay anyway, as she claims he will quiet down in a little while if he knows he has to stay. That may or may not be true, and until he does quiet down, he creates a most disturbing atmosphere for others. The teacher can reassure the mother that after four or five days, he will have him stay whether he cries or not, and at that time he will be free to help him make the adjustment. Often what happens, when it is handled in this way, is that the mother and child return the following day, there are no tears whatsoever, and the child enters happily.

If at the end of four or five days, when the mother brings the child back, and if he still will not leave her, she might be invited to stay for a while, but if the mother leaves, he should be told when she is returning, and she should be conscientious in doing so.

Each case is an individual one, and the teacher will need to use his own good judgment in helping the child and mother make the necessary adjustment. However, seeking the cooperation of the mother of the child who cries on the first day, and suggesting that she wait for a few days before bringing him again makes possible a happier start for everyone.

What to Do About the Child Who Cries After Mother Has Left

Sometimes a child is quite brave about leaving his mother, and enters without crying, but a little later bursts into tears and cannot be interested in any toys nor activities, and screams so loudly, the teacher is unable to carry on, and the other children become frightened. In such a case, it might be wise to have someone from the office telephone the mother to come to get the child, or at least remain with him for a while, and then take him home early that day. Forcing the child to stay, when he is so emotionally upset certainly does not help him and, if anything, makes him feel only more frightened and insecure. Moreover, crying is highly contagious.

Needless to say, it does not help the teacher, but makes it that much harder to provide the class with a happy beginning on the first day of kindergarten. Many schools are wise enough to provide an assistant to care for the crying child until the mother can come, in order to free the kindergarten teacher to proceed with the rest of the class. This simple precaution can prevent chaos which will take much undoing!

How to Make a Good Start the First Day

The first day of kindergarten, the teacher must accomplish two things:

First, he must make the children like him and feel eager to return the following day.

Second, he must begin to set the standards for a calm, happy classroom, conducive to growth and learning.

Each teacher has his own way of "winning over the children" and making them like him. These suggestions might be helpful in setting the stage. Make sure the children know your name. Call roll as early as possible in order to get such routine matters out of the way. Explain important rules clearly but quickly. Children must understand what to do if they have to go to the toilet, why everyone must walk and not run while in school and that they must not leave the room without permission. These are extremely important safety rules, and if inculcated early can prevent accidents and disturbing incidents.

A signal, such as a chord on the piano, a chime, or a bell, is necessary in large groups, to alert all the children when everyone's attention is desired at the same time. Whatever signal you select should not be used too frequently, however, or it will lose its effectiveness and become meaningless, perhaps just when it is needed most; for a fire or air raid drill. A second signal, meaning "Stop and look, please" might also be developed in order that the important signal does not have to be used too often. Children enjoy signals, and "hear" them much better than the same directions given orally.

Play. The children will want to play with all the interesting toys they see around the room and will not want to sit for a long talk about rules during the play period, but the teacher of a large class will find it pays to cover these points quickly before letting the children go to play:

1. Every toy has its place.
2. Each toy should be put back in place before another one is taken.
3. The teacher will help, if the child forgets where a toy belongs.
4. There is not one of every kind of toy for each person so they must share and take turns.

Pictures indicating where the toys belong make it easy for the child to remember, but it will be too much to expect that every child put every toy back in place the first day. No doubt, the teacher will have a lot of picking up to do himself. As children become acquainted with the places where things belong, and feel more comfortable in this new situation, they will take pride in keeping the room in order. Good standards should be started the first day and continued throughout the year. Warm approval and standards of consideration for others are more appealing to children than "rules." Consistent standards become invisible social mores in time.

Work. Some kindergartens combine their work and play periods into one activity, with painting, crayon work, woodworking and other art and crafts being carried on at the same time as play with dolls, puzzles, matching games, sand, blocks, and other play activities. Actually the objectives of both periods are the same, for both offer the child freedom in self expression. However, with large groups, it is difficult to keep track of the activity of each child and to know that he is getting the variety of experience and skills he needs, such as cutting, pasting, driving nails and solving problems. Because of this, there are some teachers who prefer having a period devoted to "work time," when everybody makes something, and a separate period for "play time." When the children understand how to get their materials, and put them back, they may enjoy an occasional combined work and play time. They may choose either. In this case they need to put their toys or materials away before starting something else.

Freedom to change activities takes care of many behavior problems caused by differing maturity levels or by tensions which occur between playmates. At the same time it permits a child to grow in the length of time he can stay with an activity or group. This in turn provides longer work or play periods which enable the absorbed creative one to complete a satisfying activity. The teacher's sensitivity to "timing" and flexibility in adjusting to it contribute strongly to the harmonious busy-ness which can be felt in a "good" kindergarten day. The size of a class or the shortage of assistants may not provide the teacher with much opportunity for the children's freedom of choice and change during the first week or two. But his antennae should be out for the children's signals (such as restlessness, irritability or "wildness") which may clue him to the best timing for work and play periods and change of activity.

New children cannot be expected to care properly for their materials the first day of school. They need to be introduced gradually to toys and materials. If work materials are used at all the first day, it is well to limit them. Some teachers provide crayons during the play period, on the first day or two of school. Not all children will finish what they are working on at the same time. Therefore, provision should be made for those who finish before the rest. Looking at books, drawing on the chalkboard, and such other activities might be designated as things to do.

The first time that crayons are used, children should be shown where to get the crayons, and paper, how to wait for their turn, and what to do with the pictures when finished. The teacher who takes the time to discuss these points with the group the first day crayons are used, checks to make sure his directions are followed, and is consistent every time thereafter, will soon have the children capable of being quite independent, and well on their way in developing fine school habits. Often discipline and behavior problems which develop later are the result of poor guidance and training at the very beginning of the term.

Alternating activities. Children at home, before coming to kindergarten, are used to moving about almost at will. When they come to school for the first time, they are not used to having to wait for turns, sit still without talking, and other restrictions put upon them. The necessary directions should be covered quickly. Play time should comprise a big block of time. The clean up after work and play should be thorough and cheerful but not dragged out. The entire program should alternate between active and quiet activities. Quiet activities need to be kept short. It is too much to expect a five year old to sit without talking for longer than ten or fifteen minutes, especially at the beginning of the term. Quiet activities, which require extreme quiet, such as during conversation, "when only one person talks at a time", and story or singing times, "which are listening times", must be limited, and followed by something more active where the children have more freedom to move about and talk freely. The same is true of a quiet game, such as "Dog and Bone" or "Spin the Pan", when the group must be quiet and stay in place.

Learning names. The teacher will want to learn the names of
the children as quickly as possible. During the first two or three work
periods, if he writes the names of the children on their art work, it will
help him learn their names and also prevent mixups of pictures when it
is time to go home.

Sometime during the first few days the teacher might want to
teach a game, such as "Spin the Pan" (or "Spin the Hoop"), to help both
children and teacher learn each other's names.

"Spin the Pan"

The teacher calls a child's name from a list
he holds in his hand, and then spins the hoop or pan.
The child whose name is called tries to catch it before
it falls down. The teacher should keep the game moving quickly, so that all may have a turn in a short time.
Later, when the children have become acquainted with
each other, they may call the names. If someone wants
to choose a child whose name he does not know, he may
first ask, "What is your name, please?"

Story time. It has already been said that children should not be
expected to sit without talking for a very long period of time. In selecting a story for the first day, therefore, the teacher should keep this in
mind and choose one which will be short, and which will hold the attention of the entire group. Not all children have had the experience of
having a story read to them as a member of a group. Some of them
have been used to mother or some other adult reading to them individually, or with only two or three others at the most. In this case they
have been used to being up close, where they can see the pictures, and
being allowed to comment during the story. The teacher will not want
to stifle the spontaneous remarks during the story, but he will want to
develop a listening attitude for story time from the very first day. In
order to do this chairs should be arranged so that all can see, and there
should be spaces between chairs so that they are not crowded, nor uncomfortable. The teacher needs to insist on quiet before he starts,
with everyone giving his attention. Unfortunately all children will not
have had rich experiences of having stories read or told to them. Such
children will need additional help in organizing themselves for listening.
Some teachers will prefer floor sitting to chairs. This will depend upon
the teacher and the condition of the floor. It has advantages of time and
space in small areas. The teacher will need to anticipate and provide
space for wrigglers to move without discomforting or irritating neighbors

With such a beginning and a well chosen story, the period should
be a successful one, if the story is read well. The use of pause, change
of pitch, inflection, are all important in holding the interest of children.
Pictures should be held still when shown, first to one side of the group,
and then the other. Even though most children have heard such folk tales
as "The Three Bears", or "The Three Pigs", or "The Gingerbread Boy"
or "The Three Billy Goats Gruff", such stories will hold their attention

and can be read quickly. In some communities, children might need a different selection, if the above seem like "old stuff", but as a general rule, if well done, these will hold the interest of even the child who has heard them many times before.

Safety instruction. As the most common ages of children involved in traffic mishaps (according to the Traffic Safety Association of Detroit and the Detroit Police Department), is five, six, and seven years of age, it is important that kindergarteners understand about safety patrols, and policemen, and are given safety instructions early in the school year. Children are especially excited the first few days and are in a hurry to get home. In their excitement and impulsiveness they are likely to dash into the street without looking, and be hit by a car. A few words about safety on the first day of school may save a life.

Some kindergarten children have never seen a safety patrol boy or girl, and need an explanation. Having a patrol boy or girl visit the kindergarten, putting a safety belt on a kindergarten child, teaching a song about policemen, calling attention to a toy traffic signal, (made of a cardboard box and colored paper), playing safe street crossing, with children pretending to be cars and children crossing the street during rhythm time, (stopping when the music stops because that means a red light or using red stop signs), are all ways of getting this idea across the first few days of school.

Dismissal and caring for wraps. Any teacher will need to allow ample time for children to put on their wraps in preparation for going home the first day. This is particularly true for children in the kindergarten.

Even in warm weather, when they wear only sweaters or jackets, it is well to have the children start to get ready about fifteen minutes before dismissal on the first day. (Later, the time allowed for this purpose can be shortened, according to the needs of the group.) This makes it possible for mix-ups to be straightened out, pictures distributed, and the group calmed down before it is time to go home.

In cold weather and climates where children normally wear leggings, boots, scarves, mittens, and hats, children might start twenty minutes before dismissal, but should, at first, put on only snow pants and boots. Then when all have these on, the teacher might have time to read a short story or some nursery rhymes before it is time to put on their coats and other wraps, about ten minutes before dismissal. Not all children will wear boots and leggings, but in this case they can wait to get their wraps from the coatroom. "Cubby" spaces for each child's outdoor clothing eliminate confusion, whether in the kindergarten room or a separate area.

The kindergarten teacher should be sure that each child is properly buttoned up, before he leaves the room, and that he has all his wraps. By allowing plenty of time, the teacher can assist the children to do this in a relaxed atmosphere. Older girls enjoy helping in kindergarten and many schools permit this with the permission of their teacher and principal. These girls need come to help the children about ten minutes before dismissal. Kindergarten children (and their parents) should understand that kindergarteners are expected to dress themselves, but if there is something too difficult for them, someone will be glad to help.

As early as possible, kindergarten children should be taught to hang up their clothes properly. If a child does not wear snow pants, he can put his mittens in his pockets, one in each pocket, and his hat or scarf in his sleeve. If he does wear snow pants, his mittens can be put in his hat, and the hat, scarf, sweater, and anything else (except boots and coats, of course,) can be packed in his snow pants. Then instead of having six or eight items to carry he will have only three (boots, coats and legging). Boots should be buckled or looped together if possible. Use a clothespin (assorted colors later marked with names) to pair zippered boots. It might not be feasible the first day, but as soon as it is convenient, the teacher might demonstrate with one child's wraps how each item should be packed. Children will need to be reminded often at first, but will soon take pride in packing their clothes correctly, and mothers will appreciate the fact that the clothes are not always on the floor.

If parents have not labelled clothing and boots (both of them!) with the children's names, it will be well worthwhile for the teacher to do so with individual children during a work period. Parents who are cooperative about this the first week of school often forget to do it as clothes change with the seasons.

Chapter IV

A Model Day

If the children are eager to return to kindergarten the second day of school, that in itself indicates that a fine start has been made. Some take longer to adjust than others, and may feel timid about this new experience for several weeks. However, it is usually not very long before everyone is feeling at ease and entering into activities with enthusiasm. Day by day, with a warm, friendly, understanding attitude, the teacher tries to build a fine teacher-pupil relationship, and, as she does so, and the children become better acquainted with her and each other, under such conditions most fears vanish. The children enter happily into an atmosphere that is set up just for them at their level, conducive to growth and learning, but at the same time full of fun, good times, surprises, and fascinating things to discover and ask questions about.

A Glimpse into a Session

Let us look into a kindergarten for a day after the term is well under way to see what goes on later in the term. The children enter happily, and while taking off their things, talk informally to each other and to the teacher. When Johnny tells about seeing a big fire truck, and Betty shows her new doll, the teacher listens attentively but at the same time she is making a quick check to see that there are no rashes, runny eyes, colds or other symptoms of disorder. The children help themselves to books, (or toys that can be put away quickly) while waiting for the others to arrive and then all gather around the teacher for roll call, announcements, and a conversation period.

Billy shows the boxes he has brought with which he wants to make a train, and Jean explains her box is for a television set. For this they will need paste, gummed tape, string, paper, scissors, and crayons. They know where to get these things and that they may help themselves when the work period starts. Others tell news, and after a short discussion in which the teacher shows pictures or objects to stimulate the group for the work activity, he names a few children at a time to go to work. Some children have projects from the day before which they want to finish. Some help themselves to crayons and paper, others to paint, clay, wood, or other material. They chat comfortably while at the tables, but do not shout. They are free to walk about to get more materials, to bring a problem to the teacher, or to show their friends what they have accomplished, but they do not run nor walk aimlessly. This is their time to make something. They are all as busy as bees.

Those who finish before the rest know exactly what to do while waiting for the others. Some draw on the blackboard, some look at books, some work with the flannel board, the sand, the abacus, or certain other designated toys which can be put away quickly. When the signal is given, everyone stops, listens to the teacher, and in response to his request, sits down in the suggested area. Billy is invited to show his train. He explains the problem he ran into when he tried to paste the boxes together, one behind the other, and how he solved it by using string instead. He is anxious to take it home, but decides it would be nice to leave it so he can paint it tomorrow. Dorothy, who has had difficulty in using even crayons, is proud to show her picture for it is the best she has ever done, and definitely worthy of praise, because of the growth it represents, even though inferior to the work of most of the children. The painters are invited to show their work, for there is time, but the evaluation period is kept short, worthwhile, and interesting.

Two children are invited to put the paint trays away so there will be no accident of spilled paint later when everyone is moving about during clean up time. A few special jobs are given, such as sweeping up spilled sand. Then each child cleans up his work as quickly as possible, for he knows that the room should be put back in apple pie order before the next activity is started.

When the room has been tidied up, the children sit down while Edith passes the cookies she has brought, each one thanking her in English or another language if it is being taught in the kindergarten or if there are bilingual children in the group. Then they gather around the piano to sing favorite songs. Johnny sings a song which he has just made up about the steam shovel they watched yesterday, and the teacher and children sing his new song together. The girls request a turn to do a dance, and move about gracefully to the requested music, "The Blue Danube". The boys have a pony gallop, and then all together enjoy a few more rhythms to good music. It feels good to rest after that, with heads resting on arms at the tables, eyes closed, everyone quiet, and the teacher playing softly on the piano, a favorite for the rest period, Brahms' "Lullaby".

The children are anxious to try an experiment with the magnet Betty has brought to school. Seated in a circle where everyone can see, they take turns trying to pick up paper, wood, felt, bobby pins, nails, paper fasteners, milk bottle tops, paper clips, and other items, to see which ones the magnet will attract. They make two piles, those it will, and those it will not. The teacher guides the discussion, helping the children to discover, then evaluate that which they have observed.

Before play time, the teacher chooses the cashier for the kindergarten super market, in order to avoid confusion later, and then, because they have all learned to walk, not run, to select whatever toys they want, they are all invited to go at once to play. Some go immediately to the doll corner, (to dress up in dress-up clothes, set the table, fix dinner, or care for the dolls). Some start building an airplane of big blocks. Some organize a group to play lotto or another game. Others help themselves to puzzles, books, or toys. As they finish with one, they put it back in place before taking another. During the play period, the teacher is busy, observing, helping, and guiding. Ann is a sensitive child, who has to be comforted. Billy is selfish, and has to be reminded to share. Johhny is rough and a hitter and has to be calmed down. Leonard, always full of good ideas, wants a sign for the airplane, and as he watches the teacher print the words, remarks that they ought to have tickets so they can take passengers to New York.

When play time must end, the signal is again used to gain everyone's attention, and the children are asked to put away the toys, and gather for a story, Make Way for Ducklings. Julie has brought some toy ducks which look like those in the book. They will add greatly to the children's enjoyment of this favorite story. While waiting for the late comers, those who are ready are saying nursery rhymes, and finger plays, and when all are ready, comfortably seated and quiet, the story begins. The children listen attentively, not interrupting except with some spontaneous remark of enjoyment, and not disturbing others for they have learned that story time is a "listening time", and most delightful when everyone cooperates.

It is hard to believe that it is time to go home, but the session is almost over and it is time to get wraps, pictures, or other work and get ready to leave. Children find their own work, and put on their own clothes, but big girls help with "hard" things, such as sticky zippers, tight buttonholes or boots. Everyone is quiet while reminders about what to bring to school tomorrow are given, and safety precautions are recalled, and then the good byes are said. The children leave in an orderly manner, with "See you tomorrow."

This has been a happy day for everyone. However it did not just happen this way. The good habits which were evident in the smooth running of the class were built up day by day, from the first day of school. The ability of the children to initiate their own activities developed gradually. Techniques of control, setting up materials, and planning for variety all have played important roles. The ensuing chapters discuss these in detail. It is hoped that the beginning teacher will find them helpful in achieving many rewarding, smooth running days in kindergarten.

Sample Arrangements of Time

A typical program in a modern kindergarten depends to some extent upon the physical set up of the room itself. Some kindergartens are "self contained", that is, the children have their entire program in one room, under one teacher. Others have two rooms, shared by two teachers, each in a separate room for the first part of the session, and then changing to the other room at a designated time. Usually one room is for the work period, because it contains the necessary equipment and materials; and the other for music and other activities, because it contains the piano and related materials. Still others, but very few in number, have a basic self-contained room with another adjoining room used as a work room or for resting. The program in the two rooms is not as flexible as that of a self contained room, but is a financially economical arrangement because it involves only one piano, fewer work tables and other equipment.

Let us look at the program of the teacher who starts her day in the work room, then that of the one who begins in the music room, and finally that of the teacher in the self contained room.

Starting in the work room first. The length of the kindergarten session varies from school to school and city to city, and there are some kindergartens where the children have lunch and stay all day. Each would have its own arrangement of time, that which best suits that particular situation. It would be impractical to suggest a uniform schedule, but in order to have some idea of the time allotted for various activities, let us assume the session to be two and three quarter hours long, beginning at 8:30 and ending at 11:15. (A similar division could be used for the afternoon session of similar length.)

Depending upon the geographical location and season, the children will need from five to fifteen minutes for removal of wraps. Those ready early might look at books or talk informally together while waiting for the others, or perhaps engage in a quiet game.

Children are usually bursting with things to tell when they first arrive, so, after roll is taken, no matter which room they start in, they need a "news time", (often called "conversation time", "show and tell time", or "sharing time") as the first group activity of the day. Because this period must also include stimulation and discussion for the work period, it may be necessary for the teacher to limit the conversation, and ask the children who have not had turns to save their news until after the work period.

The work period in its entirety, (including conversation-stimulation, actual work, evaluation, and clean-up), takes approximately one hour except at the beginning of the term when less time is usually devoted to this activity. If there is not much time left before changing rooms, it is well to have an activity which can be terminated quickly. Saying nursery rhymes, finger plays, reviewing a newly learned song, conversing in a second language, riddles, quiz questions, number experiences, and poetry are possibilities. Usually teachers have an under standing that being a few minutes early or late for the change will not matter, but if a class has to wait outside the room for too long a time, behavior problems are likely to develop. In order to avoid this, if there is to be a delay, it is a good idea to send a child with a message to the other teacher informing him of the delay.

If a snack is to be served, it might be well to have it immediately after the change, for at that time of day it would not interfere with lunch at home. The activities for the remainder of the session should alternate between active and quiet ones. Five year olds should not be expected to sit still, without moving about nor talking, for more than ten or fifteen minutes at a time. A quiet activity, such as a story, singing, or a puppet show, should be followed by an active one, such as rhythms, play, active game, or singing game. The teacher should keep in mind that the attention span of a beginning kindergarten child is short but increases during the term. A big block of time should be devoted to the play period, especially at the first of the year. It might, therefore, be necessary to keep the other activities shorter at the beginning than later on in the term. Ample time should be allowed for the dismissal, getting completed work to take home, and departing in a calm, orderly manner.

A typical session at the beginning of the term might be divided as follows:

8:30 - 8:45	Removal of wraps, health inspection, informal conversation, looking at books, watering plants or other jobs. Roll call.
8:45 - 9:00	Conversation and stimulation for work.
9:00 - 9:30	Work period.
9:30 - 9:35	Evaluation of work.
9:35 - 9:45	Clean up.
9:45 - 9:50	Change rooms.
9:50 - 10:00	Snack and short rest period.
10:00 - 10:10	Singing and rhythms.
10:10 - 10:40	Play period, indoors or outdoors.
10:40 - 10:50	Put toys away.
10:50 - 11:05	Story time.
11:05 - 11:15	Get wraps, finished work, and prepare for dismissal. In rainy or cold weather more time would be needed for putting on boots, raincoats, or snow suits.

The above arrangement of time would not be possible nor practical in all kindergartens, for each situation is unique and each has its own characteristics (and problems) to consider. In situations where there is not a lavatory in the kindergarten for the children to use, whenever they have need, it will be necessary to allow ten or fifteen minutes for taking the children to the hall lavatory. In sessions of greater length than previously described or in kindergartens where cots are provided, a longer rest period would be desirable. Some schools have milk or juice programs, requiring a longer period for milk or juice and snacks. In all-day kindergartens, provision for a morning snack, preparation for lunch and lunch time must be included.

Whatever the program, however, it is a good idea to follow the same routine for several days, at the beginning of the term, until the children get used to understanding the proper care of toys and materials and begin to feel reasonably secure in this new situation. It is important also to have a singing period daily in order that the children will remember the songs they learn, and build up a repertoire. A new song, if short in length, could be introduced each day and reviewed often on the following days, for children enjoy singing the songs they know well. As the term gets under way, and after the children have developed good habits of caring for the room, and have learned several songs, the singing period might be skipped occasionally in order to be able to include a greater variety of activities. If the song period is omitted too often, however, the children are likely to forget the songs they have learned. For this reason, it is well to spend at least a few minutes each day reviewing recently learned songs. If the teacher is not dependent upon a piano, this might be done before the group leaves the work room, if time permits.

Although the beginning teacher will find it helpful to map out his time in this way, the program should be flexible. As children begin to initiate their own ideas, he should feel free to make the necessary changes in his plans in order to take advantage of those child-initiated ideas which have the potential of providing worthwhile learning exper- iences. For example, if, during the play period, some children make the wooden house (with blocks) of the second little pig, that might be the ideal day to have a dramatization of the "Three Little Pigs". Being given the hint that they might make the other houses so they could act out the story, and perhaps being offered a large carton for the straw house, they probably will do so eagerly, and after play time, clean up more quickly than usual in their anticipation and enthusiasm for the show. The dramatization on such a day would probably be very success- ful, even though the teacher had not made advanced plans for it. If dur- ing the work period a child makes a drum out of an oatmeal box he has brought to school, that might be the proper time to start a rhythm band. The day a child brings a cocoon to school might be the best time to change the entire plan of the work period, the new song to be taught, or rhythm to be enjoyed as the children become interested in cocoons, butterflies and moths.

The teacher needs to plan, and to plan carefully, but after some experience, can change these plans in order to take advantage of the thing that is of interest to the children at the moment. The "here and now" is important in kindergarten.

Starting in the music room first. The teacher starting in the music room first also will want to have a conversation period at the be- ginning of the day for then the children are eager to tell things that have happened since the day before. Just before the children change rooms, it is well to have an active period, because, immediately after the change they will be expected to sit quietly for the "conversation-stimulation" part of the work period. If required to sit still during two consecutive time periods, they could not be as attentive during the second or con- versation time. They need more freedom of movement after sitting for one quiet period than is possible in just walking from one room to an- other, and they need a chance to talk to each other as well.

A typical session beginning in the music room might be divided thus:

8:30 - 8:45	Removal of wraps, health inspection, informal conversation, looking at books, watering plants or other jobs. Roll call.
8:45 - 8:50	Short conversation.
8:50 - 9:05	Singing and rhythms.
9:05 - 9:35	Play period, indoors or outdoors.
9:35 - 9:45	Put toys away.
9:45 - 9:50	Change rooms.
9:50 - 10:00	Snack and short rest period.
10:00 - 10:10	Conversation and stimulation for work.
10:10 - 10:35	Work period.
10:35 - 10:40	Evaluation of work.
10:40 - 10:50	Clean up.

10:50 - 11:05 Story time.

11:05 - 11:15 Get wraps and finished work to take home, and prepare for dismissal. (In rainy or cold weather, more time would be needed for putting on boots, raincoats or leggings.)

The "self-contained" room. The teacher who has a self-contained room is more fortunate than the teachers who must change rooms, since the program can be kept much more flexible, and it is not necessary to interrupt some valuable experience in order to go into another room at a set time. At the beginning of the term, when children need a long play period, this can be provided easily. The time spent on the various activities can be lengthened or shortened as needed. A wider variety of activities can be included because all the necessary materials are readily available. There is a distinct advantage in having materials and equipment handy, ready for use at any time. If during the play period, the children need another telephone, the problem might be solved immediately by suggesting the children make one of wood and wooden wheels. Or of a cardboard box and milk tops. A sign for the "Airport", "Store", or "Fire Station", may be made right on the spot. The piano is there too, for perhaps a witches' dance for those who make witches' hats during the work period, (as a change from the usual evaluation period), or a parade for those who make American flags around Veterans' Day, or a fashion show for those who want to show the Easter bonnets they have made. During the conversation period, if it is important to clarify a concept, or elaborate on some item of discussion, it is much better to have all the kindergarten picture and reference books handy for use at just the right moment rather than have them in another room. In short, with all his supplies at his finger tips, the alert teacher can make use of them at the right time and provide richer experiences for the children.

In the self-contained room, the program might run as follows at the beginning of the term:

8:30 - 8:45   Removal of wraps, health inspection, informal conversation, looking at books, watering plants or other jobs. Roll call.

8:45 - 8:55   Conversation and stimulation for work.

8:55 - 9:20   Work period.

9:20 - 9:25   Evaluation of work.

9:25 - 9:35   Clean up.

9:35 - 9:45   Snacks and a short rest period.

9:45 - 10:05   Singing and rhythms.

10:05 - 10:40   Play period, indoors or outdoors.

10:40 - 10:50   Clean up.

10:50 - 11:05   Story period.

11:05 - 11:15   Get wraps and finished work to take home, and prepare for dismissal. (In rainy or cold weather, more time would be needed for putting on boots, raincoats or snow togs.)

After the children become familiar with the routine of kindergarten life the program may be varied in many ways, but still alternating between active and quiet activities.

It is not wise to have either the work or play period for the last activity of the day, to be certain that the room is in order before the children go home. If the play or work period is the last activity, and the children do not clean up properly, there is bound to be confusion during the dismissal preparations. If, on the other hand, there is another activity to come after the work or play period, and if they do not clean up properly, there is still time to do so before getting ready to go home, by shortening the last activity or, if necessary, by eliminating it entirely. From the very beginning the children need to learn that they do not go on to the next activity until materials and toys are properly cared for.

Most teachers like to have a story at the end of the day because of its calming effect, but there are times when a story about a certain subject fits so perfectly into the conversation at another time that it is more advantageous to have it right at that psychological moment.

As the term progresses, and the children begin to share ideas and develop the ability to do some planning, the teacher will want to step more and more into the background. He will want to allow more time for one activity and perhaps less for another on some days, according to the interests which the children develop.

Including variety in the program. A kindergarten program that is always the same, day after day, becomes monotonous for the children and the teacher as well, and often results in behavior problems. There are many ways of varying activities such as music, games, literature, and the work period; and so many possibilities in the field of health, safety, science, social science and other activities, that there is no need to have a hum-drum routine in kindergarten. Children who tend to misbehave, often improve their behavior, for they too want to be in on making butter, playing in a rhythm band, or watching a puppet show. Providing for variety and including a "highlight" (an especially fascinating project) for each day can be a big factor in the building of good behavior in the kindergarten.

The curriculum of the kindergarten needs to allow for a planned freedom that will assist the children to develop a sense of direction and responsibility for their own learning and action, that can be further developed in later grades. The chapters which follow will help the beginning teacher become familiar with the use of planned freedom.

Use of Toilet Facilities, Rest, and Snacks

Toilet facilities. The arrangement of toilet facilities varies from school to school. Some have the lavatory as part of the kindergarten unit, making it possible for the children to use it whenever they need to. Others must use the regular school lavatories, some located close by, others far down the hall. In the latter cases, ten or fifteen minutes are needed for the lavatory period. It is a distinct advantage to have the lavatory as part of the kindergarten unit. Then children can go to the toilet, and wash their hands when they need to. When the lavatory is down the hall some teachers want the children to ask before they leave the room, so that the teacher will know where each child is; some allow the children to leave one at a time, with a pass, whenever they like; some designate they may do so only during the unorganized periods; some have a special period when everyone goes. However, in an article by Dr. Lillian Gore, entitled "What is a good nursery school?", reprinted by the U. S. Department of Health, Education, and Welfare, she states that the ideal program provides for the child to use the toilet, wash his hands or get a drink of water when he needs to. Is this not the way we do as adults?

It is not pleasant to have accidents during the session, and children need to be told about the lavatory procedure as soon as possible. They should know about washing hands, using paper toweling to dry them and where to put the used paper toweling. Boys should be taught to use the urinal or lift the seat of the toilet and to be careful not to wet it. Accidents are bound to occur, however, and when they do, they should not be considered major catastrophies nor make the child unduly embarrassed. Parents should be informed when there are accidents, so they may bring dry clothes. Better yet, a set of underwear for each child, labelled with name, should be kept on hand for such emergencies, while waiting for a rescuing parent. If this is impractical, try to provide three or four spares. Understanding parents will contribute them. They should also be informed when a child has to use the toilet too frequently.

Rest periods. There is a difference of opinion about resting in kindergarten. Where children attend for all day or for long sessions, they usually have a twenty minute or longer period to rest on cots, rugs or mats. In such cases, each child should have his own, and provision made for storing and keeping them clean. In shorter sessions, children can relax and remain quiet, with heads on arms at the tables, on chairs, or on a window seat if there is one. Some teachers have children remain prone on the floor without the benefit of a floor covering but this is not particularly comfortable nor sanitary. The longer the rest period, the more completely the children relax. Even when it is not a part of the daily routine, there will be some days when children need a time of absolute quiet and a chance to relax. At first the teacher will need to help them learn how, perhaps by suggesting they make themselves "just like Raggedy Ann Dolls". The teacher can set an example by relaxing and resting himself. Children need not go to sleep and may rest with their eyes open or shut. Such rest periods can be made even more enjoyable if soft, calm music is played. This can be a valuable time of music appreciation for them. Children can quickly learn to request, "Humoresque", "Ave Maria", Brahms' "Lullaby", Brahms' "Waltz", or Shubert's "Waltz".

Snacks. It is fun to have snacks or treats in kindergarten. This can be a calm relaxing time in itself. In some schools, fruit juice, or milk is served daily. This requires time for preparation, washing hands, and serving. In others, only cookies or crackers are served, requiring much less time. Although children should wash their hands before eating, unfortunately this is not always possible with large classes where facilities are not adequate. Before parties, however, the teacher should try to make some provisions for washing hands to help children build up this good health habit.

A tray with sides, a basket, or a shallow tin box, such as hard candies come in, can be used to hold the treats, making it easy for the child to pass them without spilling. By using a tin box that has a tight fitting cover, left overs can be quickly and easily stored. Sometimes the food may be arranged in cafeteria style, each one lining up to help himself. Treats and snacks provide a chance to pause in the daily routine of things, to learn manners, to enjoy the fellowship of eating together, as well as to renew energy.

Chapter V

Problems of Management and Control

A problem sometimes confronting the beginning teacher is that of management and control. Many are so intent upon wanting the children to like them, that they are afraid to limit their freedom, and when they become wild and disorderly, they are at a loss to know what to do. Children feel more secure when they understand just what is expected of them and what the limits are. Children need to learn they cannot do exactly what they want to do when they want to do it, for there are times when certain things may hurt or bother someone else or endanger themselves. With some children the acceptance of this concept is a slow process, but it has to be learned. Even on the first day of school, the teacher may have to check the behavior of some, if the group is to start to live together comfortably.

It is not the intention of the writers to discuss the psychological aspects of control. It is assumed that the reader has already learned the worthlessness of idle threats, bribes, rewards, sarcasm, and a negative type of punishment, and has grown to realize the value of the positive approach, the importance of deserved praise, and the desirability of an educative punishment, if punishment must be administered. Once these concepts have been understood the problem then becomes that of putting them into practice. In doing so, first let us consider the responsibility of the teacher in organizing for effective classroom management.

The Teacher's Responsibility in Promoting Wholesome Behavior

If the teacher approaches children with the attitude that there is good in every child, with sincerity in wanting to help each one make an effective adjustment, and with concern to develop a fine teacher-pupil relationship, half of the battle is won. In this case the teacher will see to it that he is well prepared for the day's teaching and all that this involves. He will let the children share in the planning, will have stimulating material to keep the children interested, and will be gentle, but firm and consistent in guiding them. He will make sure that he has the attention of everyone before giving directions, and then will give these directions in clear, simple terms, using a pleasant, well modulated voice. He will anticipate difficulties which might arise and try to avoid them if possible. He will make sure that the children are seated comfortably, not crowded too close to one another. He will establish routines of organization right from the beginning so that the children will know the correct ways of doing things and the reasons behind them. He will try to keep all of his children busy and challenged with activities which will hold their interest, alternating between active and quiet activities, and not expecting the children to sit quietly for too long a period at a time. In spite of all these precautions however, he needs to realize there still will be some children who will not be able to handle themselves properly These are most likely to be the ones who bring their behavior problems to the school with them. Suggestions on working with these children will be given later.

The Child Who Misbehaves

Children can usually be directed toward more acceptable behavior through a short individual talk about what is fair, and the application of the golden rule. The child who deliberately disobeys, defies the teach er, interferes with the welfare of others, usually does not respond to individual counseling. Nevertheless, such a child also has to be correct ed. There are probably multiple reasons for his actions and the teacher must learn to know such a child in order to help him. The teacher must keep in mind each individual, but at the same time not loose sight of the majority of children who need to be protected. There is no tried and true recipe for dealing with such a child. Each case is different because the causes are different. What might work in one case might not work in another, but the aim should be to help the child want to do the right thing. It is in the acute and complicated cases that the teacher should seek assistance from psychologist or social worker.

During the indoor play or work period in kindergarten, children should be permitted to move about and talk at will, but there should be no running nor shouting. Children often need reminders concerning care of materials, taking turns, sharing equipment, and conducting themselves so as not to bother others. If a child understands what is expected of him, but still does not behave, even after an individual reminder from the teacher, he might be told that if he continues to bother others, he will be excluded from the group and he will have to sit by himself for a while. The warning might be all that is necessary. If this warning does not suffice, it is important that the teacher follow through with the punishment. Such a follow through will make him realize that this teacher means what he says, and he is likely to think twice before ignoring the warning next time. The child will realize, too, that sitting by himself for a while is not as pleasant as being a part of the group. It also might be that he needs to calm down and be alone for a while. The teacher must make sure, however, that the child understand the reasons for his punishment. Such punishment becomes educative, for he learns that if he wants to be with others, certain behavior is expected and he must behave accordingly.

During quiet activities, such as conversation, story and singing time, children must be quiet. Sometimes well planned activities are completely spoiled by only one or two children who have not learned how to listen. Learning to listen is as important as learning to talk, recognize colors or to count, as listening is required during a significant portion of the time spent in school and outside as well. How to listen is something that children should start to learn in kindergarten. This is not accomplished in one day or a week or a month. Constant reminders are necessary, but often a gesture with a smile may be enough. At the beginning of the term periods involving listening must be kept short as young children are doers not listeners. It is too much to expect that they be quiet for more than ten or fifteen minutes. Conversation is likely to be interrupted often that first day, but a good start can be made if the teacher reminds the children that we can't hear anyone when too many talk at once, and that only one talks at a time.

Little children respond to praise, but it must be deserved praise, not false flattery. Praising a child for coming in properly, before he has a chance to do anything wrong, often encourages that child to cooperate the whole day. During a quiet activity, praising those who are ready and listening, makes many other children want to be so praised. If praise does not work, the teacher might try separating problem combinations of children first, then if the disturbance continues, it might help to put the chair of the child who is creating the disturbance about two feet away from the group, and speak to him later about his actions. Complete isolation should be used only as a last resort. If used too frequently it becomes ineffective.

Each teacher has his own unique way of developing good teacher-pupil relationships and a cooperative spirit in the group. There are times when children go too far, the whole class becomes disorderly, and the teacher can not get results, even though he tries all the positive approaches he knows. At such times, the teacher should not be afraid to say, "This noise must be stopped," and to say it with emphasis. There are situations when nothing else is effective. Constant scolding, however, becomes ineffective and children soon learn to close their ears to it, just as the man who works in a boiler factory closes his ears to that noise. If not done too frequently, children pay attention when the teacher says, "No! Stop! You can not continue this racket." The teacher with experience knows this is sometimes necessary, and the beginning teacher should not have to feel guilty when she must say it.

Talking things over with the group and getting their ideas for improving certain situations can be most helpful. When children are allowed to work out rules for themselves, and understand the reasons behind them, they are much more willing to abide by them.

Punishment

If punishment becomes necessary, as has been said previously, it should be educative, help the child to realize the results of his mistakes, and make him want to change his behavior to that which is more acceptable. When a teacher slaps or spanks a child, it is not likely that she is administering an educative kind of punishment. Perhaps there are times when a child will benefit from it, but usually it is really a display of temper on the part of the adult, and a bad habit which the sensible teacher will not let himself fall into. In spite of the fact that he stands in loco parentis from a legal standpoint, and that many parents might urge him to spank their children "when they need it," it is strongly advised that the teacher refrain from any bodily punishment, for his own protection and peace of mind.

The children in the classroom have been used to differing types of treatment at home for their misbehavior, from small reminders to slaps across the face or whippings with belts. The child who is used to the latter might not at first respond to the gentle but firm voice of a teacher. He is used to a different set of communication signals. He will want to try the teacher out to see just how far he can go before the teacher really responds. The good teacher will realize there might be many problems to overcome in helping a child with this type of background. First he will have to establish rapport, get to know him and his particular culture, and how he feels about himself and others, in order to guide him as an individual.

The Importance of Getting to Know the Child

Kindergarten, probably more than any other grade level, offers an opportunity for the teacher to know each child and the child's concept of himself. It is true that most classes are far too large, and this limits the depth of understanding of each child, but in spite of this, the very nature of the program makes possible a close relationship with the child, frequent communication with him, observation of his relationships with others, and of his actions when he is by himself.

Even during the first day of kindergarten much is revealed about each child. It has already been mentioned that some children cling to their mothers and are unable to leave them. Others come gaily in, anxious to try out this new experience. A few are frightened and wide eyed. Some are meek and silent. Some are friendly from the start with both teacher and children. Some enter aggressively and start to take over. Some prefer not to enter into activities but just be onlookers.

Some of these actions reveal that a child is able to accept himself and has matured to the point that he feels sure of himself, and able to be somewhat independent. Others of these actions might disguise the true feelings of a child. The aggressive child may be even more afraid than the one who so obviously shows his fright, but, like whistling in the dark, he covers it up by bravado. The child who is meek and silent, though no trouble to the busy teacher, may have fears and anxieties carefully hidden away, and really be in more need of help from the teacher than the loud aggressive child who so often takes much of the teacher's time. The teacher must understand each one in order to know how to help him and guide him toward accepted behavior. Conferences with parents can be extremely helpful, not only in revealing more about the child but in revealing something about the parents as well.

The kindergarten teacher aims for a fine teacher-pupil relationship, in which the child feels comfortable with the teacher, and knows the teacher is one person who understands him and accepts him for what he is, a person whom he can trust, and upon whom he can rely for help whenever it is necessary. The teacher must help the child during the year so that he will feel comfortable and at ease with his classmates. Those who feel good about themselves, and others, are more effective learners who retain that learning longer.

Chapter VI

Everyday Work Materials

The usual materials for the daily work period include crayons, paint, clay, plasticene, scissors, paste, colored paper, wood and nails. No experienced teacher would have them all available at the same time without first giving instruction as to their care, use, and the manner in which the children are to get them, use them and put them away. It is advisable to introduce each activity one at a time, and it may be several weeks before all of the activities are underway during the work period. Before considering the introduction of materials in the classroom let us first consider how these materials might be maintained.

How to Maintain Materials

Each teacher develops his own system for the children's use in the care and storage of these materials. There is no one best way, rather the system has to be developed in relation to the storage space available. To be effective the system must make it possible for the children to be independent about getting and putting their things away, and orderly in doing so. Open shelves and wooden bins usually are the most adaptable.

Crayons. The boxes in which the crayons are sent to the schools last for only a short time, and, unless they are used by only a few children, it is difficult to keep the crayons in good condition. Painted coffee cans, plastic dishes, or wooden trays are more serviceable for containers. The paper need not be quite as large in size as that used for painting, but should be larger than typing paper and kept near the crayons.

Paint. Divided metal or wooden trays, such as those used for ice tea glasses, make fine trays for the paint containers. So do six-pack soft drink bottle containers. Plastic glasses, preferably of the colors of the paint, may be used for the containers, though some teachers prefer cut-down milk cartons so they may be disposed of instead of cleaned. Some paint cannot be kept more than a week or ten days before it begins to have a disagreeable odor. Odor free paint is usually labelled as such. It is an economy in the long run to buy it rather than a cheaper variety. It is a good idea to have a definite routine for mixing fresh paint each week. Having four sets of trays and cups makes it possible to have two in use, and the other two washed and ready for the next mixing. Thin, watery paint is not very appealing nor satisfying. About four level tablespoons of powder paint to a half cup of water makes a good consistency. If the container is more than half full, the brush handles will be in the paint, and the children will get it all over their hands. Therefore, it is advisable to limit the water to about one-third of a cup and add a drop or two of water when necessary.

Some teachers cover the paint table with oilcloth, which can be easily wiped off. Others have the children cover the table with newspapers. Still others use no protection at all, but have it wiped off after each use.

Paper for painting should be large enough so the children do not feel hemmed in nor confined when they paint. Easel painting might well be reserved for second term kindergarten children only, after they have acquired the technique of pressing the paint out of the brushes.

Paste. Paste will last for quite a while except in very warm weather, if oil of wintergreen is added as a preservative. Careful measuring of the proportions of water and powder paste save time in the end. When the teacher learns the exact amount of each to use for the brand of powder paste she uses, it can be done quickly and will always come out the same. Most powder paste will make good paste if these proportions are used:

> 1 part powder
> $3\frac{1}{2}$ parts water
> 2 tiny capfuls of oil of wintergreen

Children love to stir paste, and under supervision can help with the mixing. Some teachers have even taught the children to mix their own paste as jars become empty. Individual plastic refrigerator storage containers or cold cream jars make good paste jars, and half inch wide paint brushes are fine for applying paste. In order to protect the tables when paste is used, the teacher might have each student pasting get a "paste mat" to put down first. Shirt cardboards, though small, will serve the purpose, as will newspapers or old desk blotters cut in half. Some teachers have the children cover an entire table and have one or two large jars of paste in the middle, and all those who have need to paste go there. Using individual mats, however, makes it possible for a child to paste even if he is the only one in the room who wants to do so at a particular time.

Clay or plasticene. Plasticene is much easier to keep in proper condition for the children to use than clay, but there is quite a difference in the two media. Plasticene is not very firm, and of course will not harden. Clay will harden when dry, and finished articles may be painted by the children with water paint, then given a coat of shellac, or glazed and fired in a kiln if one is available. However, clay requires a great deal of care on the part of the teacher, in keeping it in proper condition for use. If children are asked to make the clay into balls, with a slight indentation in each, as they finish using it, the teacher can put a little water into each one as needed. A covered earthenware crock keeps it best. Plasticene may be kept in a covered can (such as fruit cake comes in) and does not require water. Play-doughs of many varieties are being marketed or may be prepared from common kitchen materials.

Suggestions for Introducing Work Materials

There may be occasions when not all children will be able to have a turn to paint, paste or use clay the first time each is introduced. If this is true, a good way of making sure that everyone gets a turn is to keep a "taking turn list". Opposite the child's name can be separate columns for each new activity, paint, paste, clay, and others as they come up during the year. If the teacher intends to choose eight people to paint for the first time on a Monday, he might check each name, or better yet, put a letter "M" under that column to indicate a turn on Monday. Then on a Tuesday a letter "T" for the next eight and so forth until all have had their first turn. The same may be done for pasting, clay, woodworking and eventually finger painting, or any other activity in which the number of children has to be limited.

When all have had a first turn, in each of the everyday work activities, it is no longer necessary to keep track by means of a list. After a first experience in each area children are ready to choose their own materials. The number of children who paint may be limited by putting out only a given number of paint papers each day and asking children not to paint two days in a row in order to give others a chance.

If materials and space are adequate, of course it's better to give each child an opportunity to use new materials as they are introduced.

Crayons. Crayons need little or no introduction, for most children have had some experience with them either at home, or in nursery or Sunday school, but it might be well to remind them to have only one out of the box at a time, the one they are using, and to put it back when through so that it won't roll off the table and break. Some may enjoy new uses of crayon, such as coloring with the sides of "fat" crayons.

Paint. Children need to be taught a few simple techniques before using paints for the first time: to press the paint out of the brush so it won't drip as they take it out of the cup, to put the brush back in the same color so paints won't get mixed, and to paint on one side of the paper only. If a teacher is able to mix paint daily, she may be able to let the children mix the colors on their papers any way they like, but if paint or time is limited, it is better to ask the children not to put one color on top of another color because the paint soon will become dirty looking. More children can be accommodated at a long table than at an easel where only two may paint at a time. If a table with newspapers is used, the children can fold up the newspapers at clean-up time, and leave the painted pictures on the table to dry. Some teachers hang the painted pictures up with clothes pins or place them on racks for drying, but if the table space can be spared, leaving them on the table eliminates the possibility of the wet paint dripping down on the picture and on the floor.

Fat peanut butter jars make good solid paint containers for table use.

Paste. If individual paste mats are to be used, children should be taught to put them out before pasting. Then each child should place a

jar of paste in the upper corner of the mat, on the same side as the hand
he eats with. As soon as scissors are to be used, children should be
shown how to carry them clasped in the fist with the points down and
handles up.

For the first cutting experience, children might cut out pictures
and paste them to crayon paper, or make collages by cutting pieces of
colored paper into various shapes and pasting them on paper. Children
need to be reminded to put the paste on the back of the smaller pieces
that are to be pasted on (the colored paper or picture) rather than on the
big piece of paper. Beginners are likely to paste things on the paste
mat, so children need to be helped. The teacher has to be careful that
he does not burden the children with too many rules and regulations at
first, but guides them properly as various situations arise. Children
can be taught to put the paste brush on the paste jar lid when not using
it, and then when finished to place it in a pan of water, placed in the
middle of the paste table, so it can be washed during clean-up time.
Paste sticks are often used instead of brushes. Pasted pictures can be
placed on the paint table to dry when work time is over.

<u>Clay, Playdough or Plasticene</u>. Oilcloth mats, cutting boards,
squares of asphalt tile, or shallow trays are often used to protect tables
from clay or plasticene. A shallow tray has the added advantage of keeping the clay from rolling off, but it should have an edge no deeper than a
half inch, or it will interfere with the child's movements in working his
clay. "Keep the clay on the tray" is a good rhyme and rule. If earthen
clay is used, children need to be told about rolling it into balls when
finished, and making an indentation either with a finger or a clothes pin
so the teacher may add water to keep it moist. Plasticene can be put
back as is. It is a good idea not to have the clay table too close to the
sand box, for when they are in proximity the contents of both may get
mixed together.

Chapter VII

Providing a Rich Art Program

It is hardly possible to talk about a good art program without getting into a discussion concerning teacher-directed projects versus creative activities. One of the most confusing things for the beginning teacher is to be placed under a principal who believes exclusively in one approach after having been in a class of a college professor who taught the opposite; or to be in a school where other kindergarten teachers lean in one direction, when the young teacher's training has been otherwise. Each teacher will need to establish his own philosophy concerning this if he is to be confident in himself as a teacher.

Two Schools of Thought

In spite of all that has been written, concerning the importance of creative work as it relates to good mental health, and the value of having the child solve his own problems, there are many teachers who believe they are not doing a good job unless they present a different project every day for the children to make during the work period; sometimes even with the teacher giving directions, including what to do first, second, and third, without getting any ideas from the children. The children then go to work and all make the same thing. The child who does not care to do so is asked to do it anyway. One child's work can hardly be distinguished from that of another. There are many mothers who think this is fine, that their children are learning a lot and bringing home fine work each day. The finished product and the fact that the children are covering the same ground are most important in such a philosophy.

There are other teachers who believe that it is not the finished product that is the most important thing, but that what the child derives from the experience is what really counts; and that there is more value, especially from a mental health standpoint, in allowing a child to express his feelings, through the use of paint, clay, crayons, or other media, than in teacher-directed projects, where the child has no choice. The teacher who believes this, handles his work period quite differently. He stimulates the children to want to make something, but does not expect all to make the same thing, as he realizes they are all at different levels of ability and all have different interests and needs. He guides a discussion of the proposed activity but encourages the children to think for themselves, (for example, how an Easter basket might be made out of a certain piece of paper or box), and gets many varied methods from the group. He has available for immediate use a wealth of scrap material, (not expensive, but priceless in kindergarten,) and encourages them to use these materials the way they like. He does not desert his class in a laissez-faire attitude, but guides them when necessary and volunteers certain techniques to help them over the hard spots as problems arise. Under such conditions children learn to think for themselves, and have a greater feeling of true accomplishment than those children whose work looks alike and whose teacher has done most of the thinking as well as most of the work. It permits children of varying abilities each to create something satisfying at his own level.

Having a creative work period does not mean that a teacher must eliminate all well known kindergarten projects. Children need ideas and stimulation in order to grow. However, the creative teacher does not present an idea in a teacher-directed, step-by-step manner, but encourages children to figure out how to do such projects, confines such articles to very simple ones, so that all who try may succeed, without too much assistance from the teacher, thus avoiding those which involve the use of tiny finger muscles (for the teacher knows that such muscles are not fully developed at this time). He does not insist that everyone in the class make the same item, but has paint, crayons, clay, paste, and other materials available for those who prefer them. He does not give the children patterns to trace, and realizes a poorly shaped drawing, but one which the child has made himself, is far better than one that has been traced.

During this type of creative work period the teacher is a very busy person, with many individual projects going on at the same time, challenging advanced children and encouraging immature ones, helping all to reach their maximal potentialities.

A Typical Work Period

A typical work period might include a period of about ten minutes for conversation, (including stimulation, motivation, and planning) before children get their materials and start to work, followed by about twenty-five or thirty minutes for actually working, about five minutes for evaluating what has been accomplished, and ten for a thorough clean-up.

Conversation (stimulation, etc.,)	10 min.
Actual work time	25-30 min.
Evaluation	5 min.
Clean-up	10 min.

As a general rule it takes about an hour for a complete work period. There may be times when planning may not take ten minutes; but children will become disinterested if required to sit for longer than fifteen minutes, so the beginning teacher should be careful not to extend the conversation period.

Clean-up time, however, may have to be extended, especially at the beginning of the term, until the room is entirely back in order, and the children realize what is expected. The time schedule should not be rigid. The one presented is merely suggested as a guide for the beginning teacher.

There will be some immature children with short attention spans, or others who for some reason finish their work before the rest, who will need to be kept occupied while waiting for the others to finish. In rooms where table space is limited, it may be necessary to allow only certain fill-in activities, such as playing in the sand, looking at books, and drawing on the blackboard, until the others are through. Such activities can be quickly terminated and do not involve a long time for clean-up.

Stimulation or motivation. Although the teacher will want to get ideas from the children in the stimulation period, he should not depend entirely upon them. He should have in mind possibilities which might interest most of them, so that those who have no particular ideas are stimulated and eager to go to work. At the same time he should be alert to follow up leads from the children. With experience he will learn to identify those which have possibilities for worthwhile learning situations and work projects.

Children are most enthusiastic about child-initiated ideas. The teacher must learn to evaluate them in order to select only worthwhile ones for follow-up. If the teacher suggests making a certain thing, such as an Easter basket, the majority of children will probably want to do so. If one of the boys has just visited an airport, and enthusiastically described it during the conversation period, he probably would be much more interested in drawing, painting, or constructing an airplane of wood or cardboard. The teacher should keep in mind that just because he hopes the children will make Easter baskets on a certain day is no reason why every single child will want to do so. The teacher needs to keep planning flexible.

Actual work time. While the children are at their tables working, the teacher will not want to hover over them and make them feel uncomfortable or fearful of making mistakes. He will need to feel his way, and let them do as much as possible by themselves, stepping in only to help them over hard spots or guiding them one step further; or to share in their delight.

"What a fine house. What will it need so people can see out?"

"You made a good stop light. What can you make to go with it?"

The child will feel he has thought of the idea himself, and yet the teacher has guided him into further improvement.

Children need to know that they need not worry if they make mistakes, or they will not do their best work. Freedom to make mistakes encourages growth and venturesome creativity. They need to be encouraged to try, and if their work doesn't turn out right, not to worry but to try again, and again. The story of "The Little Engine That Could" contains some good philosophy and can be referred to in such situations. In this story, the engine says, "I think I can. I think I can. I think I can." and he does succeed in pulling the broken down train into the city, while the engine who says "I cannot. I cannot. I cannot." does not even try. This delightful story can be a big help in encouraging the children to think positively and to develop the philosophy of saying, "I'm going to try." rather than "I can't." "If you say you can't, then you can't, but if you try, sometimes you surprise yourself and find you really can." is good sound advice for five year olds.

This does not mean that every child should be told to try the same things. As the teacher grows to know his children he realizes that certain ones are just not ready for a certain activity. He will want to make such children feel more secure by suggesting a simpler project in which they can succeed.

Sometimes a child says he does not want to make a certain thing because he is afraid he cannot do so. Often a little questioning by the teacher will bring the truth to light and a little reassurance that the teacher will help him if he runs into trouble will be all that is necessary to make the child eager to try.

Evaluation. The evaluation period should be kept short and interesting. It becomes very dull for a group of children to have to listen to five or six children tell about their pictures, day after day. There will be times when this procedure can be very worthwhile, and provide others with new ideas, but if carried on every day, the children will become bored and restless. The evaluation period should be varied often. One day the teacher may invite a child who has thought of and made something entirely different and unique to show his work. Another day, he might invite all the painters, when they have painted especially well, or all the boys might show their work, then another day all the girls.

Evaluation time is an excellent time to have the group help a child solve a problem.

"Billy is having trouble making the wheel stay on his car. Can someone think of another way of fastening it on?"

Often children will offer ideas the teacher has not even thought of. When there are many fine work products which ought to be shown, the teacher might occasionally ask all of them to form a line, and lead them around the various tables to see everyone's work. Such evaluation periods will hold the child's interest and be worthwhile.

Clean-up. If children are anxious to get into their next activity and enthusiastic about it, they usually will do a fine job of putting away their materials, and cleaning up the room. If they are told what is coming next and understand that it cannot be started until the room is all straightened up, they are more likely to cooperate.

From the very first work period, children need to be told how to handle their crayon pictures, painted or pasted work, so it won't stick to other pictures; reminded to put away properly their crayons, scissors, paste, and other materials; to pick up scraps and arrange the chairs.

It has already been pointed out that children should be introduced gradually to the various work materials. (See "Suggestions for Introducing Work Materials.") As children try each new media, they need to learn how to care for the supplies and materials involved and how to clean up afterward. Children are bound to forget occasionally, but if the teacher is understanding, and doesn't consider it as a major offense, she can encourage the child who has forgotten, to "Go now, please, and put it away. Next time you will remember." If he cannot find out whose work has not been cleaned up, he might have to ask the children if they know. They usually do! The next day the teacher can remind this child privately to put his work away when the others do so, during clean-up time, and then praise him if he does it well. He is likely to forget again, but soon will get into the habit and cooperate with the others. If children realize what is expected of them, and learn to take pride in the appearance of their room, high standards can be maintained and such habits will carry over into the years that follow. Once in a while, after the teacher assumes the children have developed fine clean-up habits, he may find several children who all on the same day have forgotten. If the teacher asks all the children to stand at the place where they worked, he can praise those who cleaned up nicely and quickly discover those who forgot, and then urge them to do so as quickly as possible.

Additional Art Experiences

In addition to the usual activities previously mentioned, children enjoy other ones, such as finger painting, string painting, crayon resist, buttermilk and chalk, papier-mâché and dough. These are easier to introduce later in the term, after the children have become used to the other art activities and might enjoy a change, rather than in the beginning before they have gained any art experience. There is no reason for the teacher to fear them, if he is careful about his organization of the activity, limits the number of children participating at one time, and prepares the children properly for the experience.

Finger painting. Newspapers or oilcloth should be used to cover the table and children should have some kind of protection for their clothes, either aprons which cover them well, or men's shirts with sleeves removed, buttoned down the back. It is easier for children to finger paint if they stand instead of sit. Commercially prepared finger paint is expensive, and home made finger paint is a nuisance to prepare. However, a teacher will find it very easy to use ready made laundry starch, liquid detergent, and powder paint as finger paint. A teaspoon full of liquid detergent can be added to the starch solution in order to facilitate washing hands later. Paper should be large, about the size of paint paper, and heavy enough so that it will not wear out. It is not necessary to wet it. About three tablespoons of starch are sufficient to smear on and cover the entire surface of the paper. When the children have done this, the teacher can drop on each paper, with a tongue depressor or spoon, the one or two colors of powder paint which the child selects of the three primary colors, red, yellow, or blue, or one of the binary (orange, green, purple). (If children are allowed to choose three they will do so, and find that their pictures will all be the same color, brown.) The powder paint is then smeared with the starch and children paint with their fingers, fingernails, thumbs and palms. Children need to be reminded to stop when they have the picture the way they want it to dry, or they are likely to keep painting until a hole is worn right through the paper. If children are asked to hold their hands together when walking to the wash basin, they are less likely to get paint on others. It will be necessary to move the finished picture to another spot or it will stick to the oilcloth or newspapers. Perhaps the sand table might be temporarily closed, if there is no other place to put them, and the pictures placed on newspapers covering the sand table. It is sometimes necessary to place small blocks on the corners of the pictures to prevent curling as they dry.

String painting. String painting involves dragging a string which has been dipped into paint across the paper. Ordinary paint as mixed for brush painting may be used for string painting, in fact, the brushes may be left right in the cups in order to poke the string down into the cup. If handles of gummed tape are fixed at the end of each piece of string, and kept outside the cup, the child will be able to pick up the string easily without getting his fingers full of paint. Two large pieces of tape with the ends of the string in between might be used for this purpose. The string should be kept short, about twelve inches in length, in order that it be easy for the child to handle.

Crayon resist. Crayon resist gets its name from the fact that the crayon resists the paint, and shows through. Thin paint, therefore, must be used. Children make designs or pictures with crayons, then starting at the top left side, cover the entire paper with paint until no white is showing. Children need to be reminded that if they paint over the crayon mark twice, they are likely to cover it up. The teacher must be sure the paint is extremely thin, almost watery. Many children may have turns on the same day if they use crayons at other tables and come to the paint tables only when ready to paint over the crayon design.

Buttermilk and chalk. Colored chalk takes on a phosphorescent look when used over buttermilk. (Some teachers have found milk or water works just as well, but it does not have the thick consistency that buttermilk has.) For kindergarten it seems to be more satisfactory to spread the buttermilk around on the entire paper, as one does with the starch when finger painting, though some teachers tell the children to put the buttermilk only where they intend to draw with the chalk. In either case, after the buttermilk is on the paper, colored chalk is used to make a picture or design. Children need protection for their clothes while doing this.

Collages. Collages have already been mentioned as a possibility when paste is used for the first time, as it is easy to make them and results are pleasing. This involves cutting and pasting pieces of colored paper, cloth, or thin cardboard or combinations of materials on a sheet of paper, cloth, or thin cardboard or combinations of materials on a sheet of paper, in any design whatsoever. Interesting effects can be achieved and the beginnings of form and line in art appear in an activity which is on the child's level. Later, some three dimensional designs may be attempted--cotton clouds or bunny tails, rolled or folded bits of paper, "box" buildings.

Papier-Mache. Papier-maché has so many possibilities, it is well worth the trouble of preparing it, and if kept in a covered crock with some wintergreen oil added as a preservative, a large quantity can be made at one time and kept for several months without its taking on an offensive odor. Everyone in the class might be asked to take a turn in tearing newspaper into bits about an inch square, tearing about three or four sheets at a time. This paper is then put into the crock, with just enough water to cover it, and a few dashes of wintergreen oil, and left to stand for several days or a week. By that time, it will have started to disintegrate, and if rubbed together between the hands, will be ready for use. Powder paste should be added only to that which is to be used that day, stirred in well, then squeezed through the fingers in order that it is mixed throughout. It should be moist enough to mold into shapes. Fruits, vegetables, and other food may be made and painted for use in the store or doll corner. Easter eggs, Christmas tree decorations, and puppet heads are other possibilities. The latter can be molded on a roll made of thin cardboard (about two inches long and one-half inch in diameter). Tagboard can be shaped into a roll and held in position by masking tape.

Dough. A simple recipe for preparing dough calls for one part flour and two parts salt moistened with a little water and colored with vegetable coloring. It can be kept moist for quite a few weeks in a tightly sealed plastic bag. Children use it in much the same way they use clay or plasticene.

Sponge painting. Pieces of sponge may be cut into various shapes dipped in shallow dishes of paint and then dabbed here and there on a piece of paper. Christmas wrapping paper can be made in this manner. Children enjoy just making designs this way.

Chapter VIII

Providing a Rich Music Program

There are many musical experiences possible for the five year old beside the singing and rhythms usually carried on in kindergarten. Experiments with sounds, musical bottles, water glasses tuned to the scale, listening to records, playing the piano, joining in a rhythm band, observing older children play other instruments, dancing simple dances, creating original songs, playing games with musical accompaniment, and spontaneous singing during work or play, are all worthwhile experiences and should make possible a variety of musical activities in kindergarten.

Kindergarten teachers will want to include as many as possible, but might well start with singing, rhythms, and the rhythm band and do so with confidence before trying out some of these other activities. The suggestions which follow should help the kindergarten teacher with both the standard activities and others that are of great interest and value to the kindergarten child.

Singing

Probably the first musical experience the teacher will plan will be that of the class singing together in a group. Even the first day, children who do not know each other will enjoy the fellowship of singing together if they know the songs. Many children have become acquainted with nursery rhymes before coming to school. "Mary Had a Little Lamb", "Jack and Jill", and "Humpty Dumpty" are always good ones to start with, for almost everyone knows them and will sing them with enthusiasm. Singing should be fun, and a joy to both teacher and pupils. If the teacher plays the piano well, it will be easy for him to accompany them. If, however, he plays only a little, it may be better for him to play only the melody notes, rather than make a difficult chore out of it and feel uncomfortable in playing. Many teachers prefer to sing with no accompaniment, at least part of the time.

Children are quick to sense the attitude of the teacher during music periods. The teacher with lots of enthusiasm and a love and feeling for music soon imparts that to his pupils.

How to select a new song. Probably the most important aspect about teaching a new song is that of its selection. Once in a while a beginning teacher who usually has a most successful singing period, experiences difficulty in getting a song across; and it is nothing more than the choice of song which is to blame. If care is taken in the selection, the teacher will soon build up a fine repertoire. A good melody, clever and easy words, and possibilities for action are things to look for. Unless the melody is pleasant, and the intervals easy to attain, there is no point in considering a song further. There are plenty of songs in the kindergarten song books today which do have good melodies. The words of a song should not be a burden to learn. The most successful songs are those which are very simple, often with repetition. Not every song will have possibilities for action, but those which do, such as "I'm a Little Teapot" or the old folk song "This Old Man" make them that much more interesting. Often with a little imagination the teacher will think of some gesture to go along with the song which will give it that little extra touch.

In addition to folk songs, nursery rhymes, and songs for circle games, children enjoy those about the seasons or special days, animal songs, patriotic songs, simple foreign songs, their own original songs, and songs just for fun. The more songs the teacher knows and has at his finger tips, the more successful will be his singing period, for he will then have the appropriate song ready for that psychological moment when it will go over best.

Children and pitch. For some time, it was assumed that all children had high pitched voices, but one has only to listen carefully to their talking voices to realize that some are high, some are low and some are medium. Their singing voices are the same. The teacher will not want to choose a song which goes up too high, nor down too low. A good general rule to follow is to look for songs where most of the notes are within an octave above middle C. If the teacher can transpose he may want to do so, in order to be able to use a song which has many high notes.

Even within a good range, however, the teacher will find songs that some children will sing on pitch, some will never sing on pitch, some will approximate correct pitch, and some will not sing at all. At no time should he put undue emphasis on correct pitch, and at the beginning of the term especially, he should encourage all to join in for pure enjoyment. Children do need to be reminded, however, that they have two voices, their talking and singing voices, and should be encouraged to use the latter rather than to shout the songs, or strain their voices in other ways. This does not mean they should be told to suppress their voices, but rather that each should find his "singing" voice.

The teacher can help children attain the correct pitch and improve their singing without their realizing that he is trying to do so. After the children have learned a few songs, it is helpful to play a short introduction on the piano, so all will hear the correct starting tones, and start on the same one. Hearing the tone is important in being able to reproduce it. Later on the teacher can help children sing more on pitch, without putting undue emphasis on it, by playing tone matching games, where the children as a group echo the tones the teacher sings. He might imitate the vegetable man calling out "tomatoes", then other vegetables using a different combination of sounds for each. The same can be done with children's names and colors of clothes.

There are many reasons why a child might not sing when he first comes to kindergarten, the lack of a background of music in the home, an untrained ear, not knowing how to use his singing mechanism, immaturity, a physical disability or timidity. Singling him out will not

help him overcome any of these, but will probably only embarass him
and make matters worse. Such a child needs to feel secure, that he
belongs to the group, and with patience and encouragement will usually
eventually join in.

How to write notes quickly. With the exception of certain out-
standing music books, such as The Kindergarten Book by Lilla Belle
Pitts, Mabelle Glenn and Lorrain E. Watters, The Picture Book of Songs
by Aline Dalton, Muriel Ashton and Erla Young, and Singing Fun by
Lucille Wood and Louise Scott, there are sometimes only one or two
songs in a book which the teacher will want to use. He might want to
copy the song, find an appropriate picture, and mount both on colored
paper to make his own file of favorite songs. Music can be copied quickly if a horizontal dash is used for a note in a space, and a slanting dash
used for one on a line. It is not necessary to draw a perfect round
circle for each note. To eliminate the copying of bass notes, the
teacher with a good music background might familiarize himself with a
few chords, thereby making it necessary to put only the name of the bass
chord above the melody note. It is not too important whether or not a
teacher can make up his own bass, but an explanation is given here for
those who might care to take advantage of it, for it is extremely helpful.

How to make up your own bass. In the simplest forms of music,
the most frequent chords will be those built on the first and fifth notes
of the scale, which means that in the key of C the most frequent chords
will be C major, or C-E-G, (built on the first) and G seventh, or G-B-
D-F, (built on the fifth). The majority of kindergarten songs include
only these two chords throughout the entire song. In more complicated
music, another chord might appear, a major chord built on the fourth,
which in the key of C would be F-A-C. Knowing this, the teacher need
not copy a lot of bass notes, but can soon figure out which of the three
chords is called for, and merely jot down that letter. In the bass he
will not want to play the whole chord continuously, but will break it up
into C for the first count and then E-G for the third, or play each one
individually, in order to keep the music simple as it should be for kindergarten.

The chords to be used in the simplest keys follow:

Key of	Chords to be used	Abbreviation
C (no sharps nor flats)	C Major (C-E-G)	CM
	G Seventh (G-B-D-F)	G7
	F Major (F-A-C)	FM
G (one sharp F#)	G Major (G-B-D)	GM
	D Seventh (D-F#-A-C)	D7
	C Major (C-E-G)	CM

F (one flat Bb)	F Major (F-A-C)	FM
	C Seventh (C-E-G-Bb)	C7
	Bb Major (Bb-D-F)	BbM

- -

To figure out the chords in the more complicated keys, one needs to know how to build major chords on the first and fourth note and a seventh chord on the fifth.

To form a major chord, use the first, third and fifth.

To form a seventh chord, use the first, third, fifth, and the seventh lowered a half tone. G seventh tone ordinarily would be F#, but when lowered a half tone becomes F natural making the G seventh chord G-B-D-F.

How to teach a new song. If children are eager to learn a song, they will learn it quickly. The first step, then, is to make them eager to learn it. This can be accomplished in a number of ways. If the group has become interested in some special thing, for example: a turtle, that would be the time to teach a turtle song, and the teacher need say only, "We have a song about a turtle we can learn today." Stimulating the children with the real thing, a miniature or picture of it, or an accompanying action are some of the ways of doing this. New words or concepts should be explained, if necessary, so that children understand what they are singing.

According to our present theories of learning, the song should be taught as a whole, rather than in parts. Only rarely, with exceptionally long songs should it be necessary to take out a difficult part for special practice.

Whether or not the teacher should use the piano when teaching a song for the first time has been discussed pro and con on many occasions. Some feel the children hear the tones and the words better when no accompaniment is used. If, however, the teacher needs the help of the piano to guide him, it would be better to use it, than to have the children hear wrong notes. Generally it is better to sing the words, rather than say them, so the children can learn both the words and the melody at the same time. Sometimes, however, there are some kindergarten teachers who feel their voices are not adequate and are unable to stay on key. It may be better for them to say the words, and teach the melody by playing the piano.

When a piano is used, it should be so placed that the teacher is able to see all the children even while playing, and he should train himself to keep his attention on the children, and not concentrate entirely on playing the piano. If children seem only half interested and become disinterested, he might well analyze his preparation, stimulation and manner. Most children thoroughly enjoy singing together, yet often the beginning teacher gives up too soon and loses confidence in himself. The experienced teacher realizes that children must learn to listen during singing time, or even the best planned lesson is spoiled. He does not expect them to remain for too long a period, but he does insist on quiet, and moves quickly from one song to another. If children have to wait, while he looks up the song, or turns pages, they become bored.

How to encourage children to create songs. Children do not need much encouragement to create songs, for they are doing so almost all the time as they sing to themselves during play, or chant phrases together. The problem is that of recording the song, in order that it can become a part of their repertoire. During work or play, if a song develops, the teacher might praise the child for the song he has made up and ask him to come to the piano to help write it down. The teacher with little music background will find it difficult at first to determine the notes, but with a little practice, he will be able to arrive at a reasonable facsimile of the child's melody. Instead of trying to write it out on music paper, if he can find the notes on the piano, and jot down their letters above the corresponding words, he will be able to record more quickly.

Often a lovely melody, such as that in the folk song, "Tirra, Lirra, Lirra" can be used for another season of the year if children make up appropriate words. A discussion about how they enjoyed that song in the spring, and how it might be changed into a fall song will bring forth several ideas, and with a little help from the teacher can become a favorite song.

Though the most worthwhile songs are those created spontaneously, the teacher might want to ask the group to think about a certain subject with the definite purpose of making up a song about it. Sometimes just this type of discussion will bring forth ideas, or perhaps the teacher will want to show a picture in order to suggest possibilities. Once the idea takes hold, the teacher will be swamped with young song writers.

Body Rhythms

Teachers might find it helpful, in their own thinking, to classify rhythms in this way:

Fundamental - consisting of marching, running, skipping, galloping, hopping, jumping.

Interpretive - consisting of those activities in which the child is imitating his surroundings, such as the postman, an animal, a boat, and so forth.

Creative - consisting of those activities the child creates out of his own imagination and experience, such as raindrops, the wind, sleepiness, seeds growing, happiness.

The kindergarten teacher will want to include all of these during the year, but will find his first rhythm activities more successful if he starts out with those which are most familiar to the children. Not all children are able to skip or gallop when they come to kindergarten, but all can walk, run, or jump, pretend they are driving cars, pretend they are dogs, and so forth and the majority will enter happily into such activities even the first day. There will be some who prefer to watch and should be allowed to do so. Eventually the teacher can usually get such students to participate by asking the group to get partners and by making sure the onlooker is chosen quickly. Providing a rhythm in which these children are especially interested, such as being airplanes, horses or road-building machinery is another way of tempting them into the fold.

As in singing, the teacher will need to keep his children in view and in mind, if he uses the piano during rhythms. A fine pianist can add a great deal to the activity, but even the best player will sometimes want to make use of the record player and instruments such as the drum, tambourine, xylophone, triangle and others. There are definite advantages in the use of these instruments as the teacher can actually be a part of the group, participating and moving about with them instead of being stationed in one place playing the piano.

The use of percussion instruments for accompaniment. The teacher without any musical background at all can employ instruments such as drums or triangles successfully, if he counts to himself properly, and accents the proper beats, as underlined below:

Walk	Count evenly, "1 2 1 2" or, "1 2 3 4 1 2 3 4"
Run	Count quickly and evenly "1 and 2 and 3 and 4 and"
Skip	Count the numbers evenly, but with a quick "da" before each one. " 1 da2 da3 da4, da1 da2 da3 da4 da"
Gallop	Count as for the skip or count evenly "1 2 3 4 5 6 1 2 3 4 5 6"
Waltz	Count evenly "1 2 3 1 2 3 1 2 3 1 2 3"

The accents are extremely important not only in playing instruments for rhythms, but in playing the piano as well. The children will get the rhythm much more quickly if the accents are exaggerated slightly, for they will be able to feel it more strongly.

By using a little imagination, the teacher can use the instruments in many ways. A few examples follow:

Rhythm	Instruments Used	How to use
Falling leaves	Xylophone	Go down scale slowly
Walking through leaves	Xylophone Drum Triangle	Beat walking rhythm
Squirrels running	Xylophone	Beat running rhythm on one or two low notes. Go up the scale when squirrel goes up the tree.

Raking leaves	Xylophone Triangle	Beat waltz rhythm "1 2 3 1 2 3".
Seeds growing	Xylophone	Go up scale, slowly, evenly.
Raindrops	Xylophone	Go down the scale with short quick beats.
Roller skating	Xylophone	Beat waltz rhythm.

Variations of Movements

The rhythms mentioned so far have involved movements of loco-motion. Non-locomotor movements, involving swinging, swaying, rock-ing, bending, reaching, twisting, stretching, turning in place, are also part of rhythms.

After some initial experiences children generally enjoy thinking up different movements themselves, and if given an opportunity to demon-strate individually the ones they have thought of they will produce most unusual ones. These individual experiences might be followed by letting as many children as possible move around the room in any way they like as long as they do not bump into anyone else.

A number of variations of the fundamental rhythms may be used by changing the direction, (going backward, sideward), changing the level, (for example walking like a hunter, stealing through the woods,) changing focus (for example, walking on toes, trying to see a bird in a tree), or changing foot positions, (walking pigeon toed like a penguin, or toes out like a duck.)

Dances. When children have become conscious of various move-ments they might employ, they enjoy making up their own dances. They might do these movements to certain music, or they might create a dance about a definite subject, and develop movements to do in the be-ginning, middle and end of the dance. A dance about Jack Frost might have for its beginning tip toe movements as Jack is looking for someone to pinch; for the middle, short quick movements as he pinches people's toes and noses; and for the ending, running away silently on tiptoes laugh-ing to himself. In addition, children can learn simple dances such as "Badger Gavotte", "I See You", "Will You Dance My Partner?"

Kindergarten children are not able to do a complicated square dance as adults do and keep in square formation, but they are able to dance with partners, and follow the call for such movements as: Bow to your partner, Swing your partner, Promenade your partner, Girls go around the boys, Boys go around the girls, Slide with your partner, Skip with your partner, and other simple routines. After showing the children what they should do for each call, he might have one or two couples de-monstrate for the others while he plays the piano and gives the call. When all understand, more couples can be invited to join in the dance until the entire class is dancing.

Discovering Sounds

Sound is such an important part of music, that the more the child is encouraged to notice sound, the better will be his music background. Taking the time to discuss and imitate the sounds children can hear in the schoolroom, on a farm, at the zoo, can be a worthwhile musical experience. Tapping with a stick various articles about the room, and bringing to school articles which make different sounds make children sound-conscious and stimulate them to discover more sounds and to be more aware of the possibilities of producing sound.

If a teacher is fortunate enough to have a room large enough to house a rack of hanging musical bottles he can easily make them by filling eight medicine bottles with varying amounts of water (to sound like the notes of the scale), and then sealing them tightly. The amount of water is varied until the proper sound is produced. Coloring may be added to make each a different color in order that children may "read" the music of colored notes.

Children enjoy making drums of oatmeal boxes, by painting them or covering them with colored paper, and then playing them during play time or with the rhythm band. Rattles of small boxes, (in which sand, beans, pebbles, or stones are sealed), and clappers made of wood and bottle caps are other possibilities.

The Rhythm Band

There are many ways of providing rhythm band experiences for five year olds. Some teachers like to use just a few instruments at a time, having only a few children play. Others like to have everyone with an instrument so that all may take part. If thirty or thirty-five children are playing at one time, however, the teacher must consider the sound that will be produced and provide the proper proportion of "soft" instruments so that the result will be pleasing music and not just plain noise.

Children should be told the name of each instrument if they do not already know it, how to hold and play each one, and how to hold it so it won't make noise in between numbers and when directions are being given. Children will want some time to experiment and hear the sounds produced by the instruments before they play together as a group. This can take place for a few at a time while others choose their instruments Children need to learn to keep their instruments quiet between numbers or they will not be able to hear directions from the teacher.

A few records are available for use with a rhythm band, but if the teacher plays the piano, he will find that much more satisfactory. By using a piano he will be able to accent properly, separate the notes, and play at the appropriate tempo.

There is no point in using any old melody when children can be exposed to fine music by good composers just as easily. Shubert, Mendelssohn, Grieg, Schumann, Gounod, Strauss, Tchaikovsky and many other have all written beautiful music, some of which has been simplified for use in the kindergarten.

There are many different ways of varying the rhythm band experiences. Children may play softly when the piano plays softly, and loudly when the piano plays loudly; they may be divided into two or three groups, with each group playing only when their group is called; or, when they have become very familiar with the music, instead of beating a steady rhythm, they might beat the value of the melody notes, or children might be encouraged to give their suggestions for playing a certain piece. If the rhythm band is to be a truly worthwhile musical experience it should not be used for show only, but should help children appreciate and become familiar with good music, the dynamics, note evaluation, and phrasing; and provide a first hand experience of actual participation and creation.

If a teacher has had a good music background he may know how to prepare bells for a "Bell Band." To do this ordinary bells used to decorate Christmas packages may be mounted on clothespins or tied with wire for a handle, all bells of one particular pitch being designated by a specific color. Christmas songs sound particularly charming with such an accompaniment. The teacher can call out a particular color to play at that time, changing the tones by calling different colors throughout the piece.

Chapter IX

Language and Literature

The kindergarten, more than any other grade, provides possibilities for a well integrated language arts program. In fact the entire program is an integration of all subjects. Social studies, mathematics, science and others, at some time or other, run through all the activities, such as art, music, dramatic play, games and literature.

Language seems more closely related to literature than other subject areas, so will be included here, though, of course it permeates every other activity as well. Those activities which promote language development, other than the obvious conversation or sharing period, include puppet shows, dramatizations, the story period, and other activities which promote language and thought.

Puppet Shows

A simple puppet stage can be made out of a large carton in which paper towels are packed, by cutting out the entire back, and making an opening in the front. It can be painted, or covered with adhesive-backed paper to make it more attractive. The same stage may be used for a television set, and by stretching a sheet across the front opening, may also be used for shadow puppets.

Shadow puppets. Old umbrella spokes are good to use for the sticks to which cardboard figures are attached with scotch tape to make shadow puppets. Those with movable arms, operated by moving the stick attached to the arm, make them very fascinating, but simple ones are just as satisfactory. Scenery may be included by pinning an appropriate shadow to the sheet. An ordinary lamp with the shade tilted to confine the rays to the area of the screen is all that is necessary for lighting. This lamp is placed in back of the sheet, about two or three feet away. Puppets are held behind and close to the sheet. In this way a shadow is cast, which the audience sees on the other side. Children may operate nursery rhyme characters, but because the verses are over so quickly a familiar story such as "The Three Billy Goats Gruff", "The Three Little Pigs,", or "The Three Bears" seems more satisfactory. The teacher might want to be the "narrator", with the children talking for the puppets, until the children are able to do the entire skit by themselves.

Hand puppets. At first the children may need a few ideas from the teacher as to what the puppets might discuss or do, for example, discuss safety rules, or Halloween, say nursery rhymes or sing a song or two. Later they will be able to plan their own shows and present them to the group, with only a little guidance needed from the teacher. Children should be discouraged, however, from having their puppets aimless ly hitting the other puppets, and should be helped to think up worthwhile ideas for puppet shows. A show put on by the teacher is a real treat if well done. A familiar story or an idea he wants to convey can be most effective through puppetry. Puppets are not expensive to buy nor to make. Home made ones can be made by using cotton for the head, covered with cloth or felt, pad-shaping it around a roll of cardboard for the middle finger, or placing the head on a wooden spoon. Sock puppets may be made of socks, with cardboard inside, to be operated like a mitten. Because moths are likely to get into woolen materials, it is better not to use them. Cotton felt, instead of wool felt, should be used.

Dramatizations

Familiar stories, such as "The Three Pigs," "The Three Bears," or "The Three Billy Goats Gruff" are simple and easy for the children to act out. Stories with lots of characters or scenes do not seem to work out as well. Simple costumes, such as head bands with ears for the bears, and hair for Goldilocks, ears for the pigs and the wolf, and horns of different sizes for the three goats add a great deal. Children can be encouraged to think up other props which might be used, such as the dishes and table from the doll corner for "The Three Bears," blocks for a bridge for the goats, and so on. The children speak the various parts with the teacher acting as narrator, helping the children know when and what to speak.

Sometimes a usually timid, quiet child will surprise even the teacher by his ability to participate before the group in such an activity. Though it is important to give all who want a turn a chance to play a part, the teacher will want to choose those who can be depended upon to speak up loudly and clearly for the first attempt. Children will need the help of the teacher in discussing the play a little before hand, and in narrating the story during the performance. Dramatizations should be kept simple and short, and not made into elaborate productions.

Stories

A complete list of good stories for kindergarten children would be far too long and too soon out of date to make it practical to include an extensive list. However, a number of those that are especially of interest to children have been included to illustrate different ways of presenting stories. These will help the kindergarten teacher provide a variety of experiences.

By the teacher. One of the most enjoyable and valuable activities in kindergarten is story time when a story is read by the teacher. Children love it for its entertainment and pleasure, and at the same time, build up a love for books and a desire to learn to read and find out for themselves. New concepts are developed, vocabulary is increased, correct pronounciation is learned, a fund of information is built up for future reading, and the importance of the printed word is realized, all of which are important aspects of the reading readiness program of the kindergarten.

Care must be taken in the selection of the story, however, or the group will be inattentive and the experience of little value. Children love stories about animals, transportation, everyday experiences, and nonsense. They enjoy repetition, such as is found in the old folk tales, "The Three Bears," "The Three Pigs," "Chicken Little," The Gingerbread Boy," and "The Three Billy Goats Gruff." At the beginning of the term, the teacher will want to select rather short stories, those appropriate for this level, and those with exciting plots, which will hold the interest of the group for the entire period. Folk tales are especially good at this point.

Sometimes children bring books from home, which they expect the teacher to read. Although some may be excellent, others may be very inappropriate, beyond the level of the group, poorly written, and not even good literature. It is best not to read such books, but instead, let the children show them, and share the pictures with the others during play time, explaining kindly that that particular book is better for home than school. Good books live a long time. "The Tale of Peter Rabbit" by Beatrix Potter was published in 1902 and is still a favorite.

The kindergarten teacher will want to keep abreast of good, newly published books, but will find that children love to hear over and over again the following:

Bragg, Mabel Caroline. The Pony Engine. New York: Platt and Monk Company, 1954. Unpaged.

Burton, Virginia Lee. Katy and the Big Snow. Boston: Houghton Mifflin Company, 1943. 32 pp.

Burton, Virginia Lee. Mike Mulligan and His Steam Shovel. Boston: Houghton Mifflin Company, 1939. 48 pp.

Dines, Glen. The Useful Dragon of Sam Ling Toy. New York: The MacMillan Company, 1956. Unpaged.

Esphyr, Slobodkina. Caps for Sale. New York: W. R. Scott, 1947. 42 pp.

Fatio, Louise. The Happy Lion. New York: Whittlesey House, 1954. Unpaged.

Flack, Marjorie. Ask Mr. Bear. New York: The Macmillan Company, 1932. 32 pp.

Flack, Marjorie. Wait for William. Boston: Houghton Mifflin Company, 1935. 33 pp.

Flack, Marjorie and Kurt Wiese. The Story About Ping. New York: The Viking Press, 1933. 32 pp.

Gág, Wanda. Millions of Cats. New York: Coward-McCann, Inc., 1928 32 pp.

Geisel, Theodor Seuss. The Cat in the Hat. New York: Random House, 1957. 61 pp.

Heyward, Du Bose. The Country Bunny and the Little Gold Shoes. Boston and New York: Houghton Mifflin Company, 1939. 48 pp.

Lamorisse, Albert. The Red Balloon. Garden City, New York: Doubleday, 1957. Unpaged.

McCloskey, Robert. Blueberries for Sal. New York: The Viking Press,
    1948. 54 pp.
McCloskey, Robert. Make Way for Ducklings. New York: The Viking
    Press, 1941. 67 pp.
Payne, Emmy. Katy No-pocket. Boston: Houghton Mifflin Company,
    1944. 32 pp.
Potter, Beatrix, The Tale of Peter Rabbit. 1st printing Private. 2nd
    Printing, Frederick Warne, 1902.
Rey, Hans Augusto. Curious George. Boston: Houghton Mifflin Company,
    1941. 55 pp.
Tworkov, Jack. The Camel Who Took a Walk. New York: Aladdin
    Books, 1951. 32 pp.
Ward, Lynd. The Biggest Bear. Boston: Houghton Mifflin Company,
    1952. 84 pp.

Children should be comfortably seated for the story, and not fac-
ing windows for it is not good for their eyes to face the light for an extended period of time. All should be able to see, and as close as possible to the teacher without being crowded. Before starting, the children
should be absolutely quiet and attentive with hands in their laps. The
book should be in good condition. A few preliminary remarks about the
book, its author, and its lovely illustrations will help children appreciate good books and fine authors, and to develop the concept that the
book was actually created by a person. If the teacher is enthusiastic
about the book, the children will be also. Children like to see pictures
as the story is being read. If the book is held to one side, and then to
the other side, the teacher can show the pictures and read at the same
time. If the top of the book is tipped slightly forward the pictures can
be seen more easily. Rather than have the picture in constant motion
by moving it slowly from side to side, it is better to hold the picture
still, first for one side of the group to see and then for the other.

The reader must be familiar with the story. He should know it
well enough to take his eyes off the print frequently in order to maintain
eye contact with the children.

The book should be one that can be read in one sitting, except in
rare cases, such as The Country Bunny and the Little Golden Shoes by
DuBose Heyward. This beautiful story is rather long for kindergarten
at one sitting. However, there is a very natural point at which it may
be divided, and the remainder read the following day. As a general
rule, reading stories in installments does not prove satisfactory.

Children enjoy visual aids with the story. Toy animals, or better yet, the real animal itself, other toys, such as a toy steam shovel
for Mike Mulligan and the Steam Shovel, or other objects, such as odd
mittens for One Mitten Lewis are good attention getters. To avoid interrupting the story too often, it is wise to explain new concepts before
starting, so that children have a chance to discuss them. "Does anyone
know what a snow plow is?" "This is a story about a snow plow just like
the one Billy told us about."

Although the reader should not overact and exaggerate the drama-
tics of the story, neither should he read it mechanically, without thought
as to the meaning. Proper use of inflection within a sentence, and within

a word, pauses, change of pitch, and timing are important techniques of dramatic art which can be used to enhance the enjoyment of the story. If the story is read with expression, the children will feel the emotions the author hopes to convey: sadness, happiness, or suspense. A slow tempo for sadness, a quick tempo for light gay parts, pauses for building up suspense or to let an idea sink in, and emphasis of key words, all help to put the story over. Facial expression too can be an aid. The voice, well modulated, should be loud enough for all to hear. Correct pronounciation and good articulation should be an example for the children at all times.

Good listening habits should be cultivated from the beginning. If too many spontaneous remarks are made, the teacher might suggest that for the rest of the story, the children just listen. If one or two disturb by talking to each other, an eye to eye smile, a signal with the finger over the lips, or directing a question about the plot usually will stop them. One or two children should not be allowed to spoil the story for the others. If children continue to disturb, it may be necessary to change their places to spots where they will listen better, possibly next to a very quiet child.

Most stories are read for the pleasure they give, and it is not necessary to have an evaluation after each one; but in some cases, a discussion is very worthwhile.

"Are there really any witches?"

"No, but it makes a good story, doesn't it?"

"Could animals really talk and do those things?"

"How else might the story have ended?"

"Does your story of the 'Gingerbread Boy' end like this?"

If the teacher knows a few stories well, such as the familiar folk tales, and is able to tell them rather than read them, he will find many opportunities to make use of this talent. When there is not time for a full story period, or while the class is waiting because of an unexpected delay of some kind, this ability is very helpful.

Some people feel that folk tales should always be told, not read. The beginning teacher may find this difficult at first, but after a few readings of a specific story will know it by heart and have no trouble. Being able to tell such stories, he can make better use of visual aids, such as those mentioned before: puppets, and the felt board.

By the children. Some children are able to tell certain familiar stories, and, with the help of illustrations, even more difficult ones. Being able to tell of events in proper sequence shows desired growth in language and thought.

With film strips. Most Boards of Education maintain libraries of audio-visual material, including film strips, and educational films. If quite a bit of effort is involved in obtaining the projector and screen, and if the films are very short, it is well to show two related ones at one time. Children might have a little stretch and freedom to talk while the teacher is changing films, but will not mind at all sitting for a "double feature."

With glass slides. Glass slides, three by four inches, can be made either with special crayon for glass slides or with India ink. If made with crayon, it is necessary to draw on frosted glass, and cover with clear glass, binding the edges of the two pieces of glass together with tape. If India ink is used, it is not necessary to use a cover glass. Detailed drawings are not necessary, as glass slides project best when slides are simple but clear. Often a talented parent will enjoy making these.

With pictures, cards or books in the opaque projector. Some books have such small pictures that the only way the class can truly enjoy them is to see them projected by means of an opaque projector. Christmas, or other holiday cards, may be used in this way to encourage children to create their own stories, and children can be given paper which will fit into the projector for the express purpose of making pictures to show on the screen. Opaque projectors very reasonable in price have just recently appeared on the market which make the use of this device much more rewarding. Children who have demonstrated some ability in art might be asked to make pictures for various scenes of a familiar story, or all children might make pictures or designs just to be able to see them "blown up," as they appear when projected.

With a felt board. The artistic teacher will find it easy to make felt designs to illustrate stories, but even the teacher with very little talent can trace pictures onto felt. In some cities teachers may order felt boards and cut outs from the audio-visual center or museum. Home made felt boards can be made from either felt or flannel mounted on a frame or tacked to the bulletin board. Pictures or other cut outs can be made from felt or flannel. Some teachers cut out pictures from magazines and other sources and then paste small pieces of sandpaper on back of the picture to provide the adhesive factor. Another innovation is to make the cut outs directly from colored paper toweling. These and many more combinations can be used by the creative teacher in "felt board work. "

Poetry

Besides the nursery rhymes and finger plays commonly used in kindergarten, there are many lovely poems suitable for the five year old. Sometimes, they are not used because the teacher is not sure just how to present them. If the teacher is familiar with at least the subjects of several poems, he will find them invaluable for use at that psychological moment when that particular subject is brought up.

Poems. There will be some poems the children will want to learn, others which they will just want to hear occasionally. If they are taught, they should be taught as a whole, by frequent repetition, until all are able to say them along with the teacher. With longer poems, or children who have difficulty in memorizing, the teacher might find it helpful to read a line himself and then have the children repeat that line after him in unison.

Children need a certain amount of preparation for poetry. They need to understand that poems are different from stories, and should be encouraged to discover for themselves what that difference is. Often children speak poetically, without realizing it, as the child who walking through the dry fall leaves remarked,

> "Crickety, Crickety!
> Crickety, Crickety!
> Crickety go the leaves."

If the teacher records such poems, they will enjoy saying them together, because they will be their very own. The children might be asked to sing the words. Thus, a song will have been created.

Some poems will need to be read slowly, in order for the meaning to be clear, and again the use of inflection, change of pitch, pause, and timing, as in story-telling, are important in interpreting them.

Finger Plays. Children love to do finger plays. These plays are good to use as attention devices when children gather for a group discussion or listening period. If a teacher starts a finger play, rather than calling the names of children who are not listening, he will find that he can gain their attention quickly and in a more pleasant manner through enticing them to join in the activity. New finger plays which the children have not yet learned by heart are especially good at such times. Many of the finger plays are concerned with special days, but if there are none for a certain holiday or subject, the creative teacher can easily make them up. Some of the author's favorites are:

FIVE LITTLE SQUIRRELS

Five little squirrels, sitting on a tree.
The first one said, "What do I see?"
The second one said, "I smell a gun."
The third one said, "Oh, boy, let's run."
The fourth one said, "I'm not afraid."
The fifth one said, "Let's hide in the shade."
Bang went the gun (clap hands) and away they did run. (everyone.)

FIVE LITTLE FROGGIES

Here are five little froggies.
The first little froggie broke his toe.
The second little froggie cried out, "Oh!"
The third little froggie laughed and was glad.
The fourth little froggie cried and was sad.
The fifth little froggie, so thoughtful and good,
Hopped to the doctor as fast as he could.

HERE'S A BALL FOR BABY

Here's a ball for baby, big and fat and round. (hands shape ball)
This is baby's hammer, see how he can pound. (hammer fists together)
These are baby's soldiers, standing in a row.
This is baby's music, clapping, clapping so.
This baby's trumpet, toot, toot-toot, toot-toot.
This is how baby likes to play at peek-a-boo.
This is baby's umbrella to keep dear baby dry.
This is baby's cradle, rock a baby bye.

TELEPHONE POLES

Here are two big telephone poles.
Between them a wire is strung.
Two little birdies hopped right on
And swung, and swung, and swung.
(Hold up first fingers for poles; middle fingers meet for wire; let thumbs
rest on top for birds)

TWO LITTLE DICKIE BIRDS

Two little dickie birds sitting on a wall.
One named Peter, one named Paul.
Fly away Peter. Fly away Paul.
Come back Peter. Come back Paul.

MOTHER'S KNIVES AND FORKS

Here are mother's knives and forks.
Here is father's table.
This is sister's looking glass.
And this is the baby's cradle.

EENCY-WEENCY SPIDER

Eency-weency spider went up the water spout.
Down came the rain and washed the spider out.
Out came the sun, and dried up all the rain,
And the eency-weency spider went up the spout again.
(Crawl fingers of one hand up arm (upright)
Flutter fingers downward as rain.
Circle arms in front of face, fingertips touching (as sun).
Repeat spider crawling up spout.)

CHURCH

Here is the church. Here is the steeple.
Open the door and see all of the people.
(Dramatize with hands)

TEN LITTLE SOLDIERS

Ten little soldiers, standing in a row.
They all bowed down to the captain, so.
They marched to the left, and they marched to the right.
They stood in line all ready to fight.
Along came a man with a great big gun.
Bang went the gun, and away they did run.

FIVE LITTLE SOLDIERS

Five little soldiers, standing in a row.
Three stood straight, and two stood so.
Along marched the captain, and what do you think?
Up jumped the soldiers, quick as a wink.

HERE IS THE BEEHIVE

Here is the beehive. (right hand cupped inside left hand)
But where are the bees?
Hiding inside, where nobody sees.
They're coming out now. They're all alive.
One, two, three, four, five. (lift each finger as counting)
Bzzzzzzzzzzzzzzzzzzzzzz.

FIVE LITTLE JACK-O-LANTERNS

Five little Jack-o-lanterns, sitting on a gate.
The first one said, "My, it's getting late."
The second one said, "Ghosts are in the air."
The third one said, "Who goes there?"
The fourth one said, "We'd better run."
The fifth one said, "It's just Halloween fun."
Puff went the wind. Out went the light.
And away went the Jack-o-lanterns on Hallowe'en night.

FIVE FAT TURKEYS

Five fat turkeys, sitting on a fence.
The first one said, "My, am I immense!"
The second one said, "I can gobble at you."
The third one said, "I can gobble too."
The fourth one said, "I can spread my tail."
The fifth one said, "Don't catch it on a nail."
The farmer came along and stopped to say,
"Turkeys look best on Thanksgiving Day."

FIVE LITTLE REINDEER

Five little reindeer, prancing in the snow.
The first one said, "When is Christmas? Do you know?"
The second one said, "I think it must be soon."
The third one said, "I heard a Christmas tune."
The fourth one said, "There is Santa at our sleigh."
The fifth one said, "Then tomorrow is the day!"
Let's all line up and be ready for the flight
For this must be Christmas Eve tonight."

DON'T YOU THINK I'M GETTING WISE?

This is East and this is West
Soon I'll learn to say the rest.
This is High and this is Low
Only to see how much I know.
This is Narrow; this is Wide.
See how much I know beside.
Down is where my feet you see.
Up is where my head should be.
Here is my nose and there, my eyes.
Don't you think I'm getting wise?
Now my eyes will Open keep
But I Shut them when I sleep.

Other Activities Promoting Language and Thought

Children enjoy games involving thinking, if they are simple
enough for them to realize success in playing. The kind of question
asked would depend, of course, on the group, their home backgrounds,
and the experiences they have had together. There are many possibilities.

Quiz games. Simple questions or riddles, based on previous
group experiences, such as "Name five vegetables," "What nursery
rhyme is about an egg?", or "I went into Mr. McGregor's garden. Who
am I?" can be printed on small pieces of colored paper and a child
chosen to draw one of the questions. If unable to answer the question,
the others might be asked to help him. It is fun to have a make-believe
prize, such as "a big red fire engine" or "a doll that talks", if the child
answers correctly.

Panels. Four or five children may be asked to be on a panel to
discuss such questions as "What would you do if you lost your mother in
a downtown store?" or "Why should children not play with matches?" or
to discuss some current problem of the group, such as "What can we do
so that more children will have a chance to ride the horses everyday?"
Questions which have several possible answers encourage children to
think individually to solve problems.

Thought games. Asking the group to think of words which rhyme
or words which mean the opposite of certain ones, (such as big-little,
dirty-clean, old-new, hot-cold), or to think of all the round things in
the room, all the things that go on wheels, or all the things in their
homes which run by electricity are possibilities.

Counting games. A felt board lends itself most advantageously
for counting. Leaves or apples for a tree, Easter eggs, or balls may
be counted. Suggestions for their use and other counting games are
given in the chapter on "Mathematics" under "Number experiences and
songs."

Television shows. Children who might be too timid to get up before the group often feel quite secure behind a television screen, which

can be made out of a large carton.   Stories, poems, songs, weather reports and even commercials are likely to be given if children are given
an opportunity to make their own suggestions for a TV show.

Chapter X

The Play Period

Children need companionship, not only of those the same age as they are, but also of those a little older and a little younger. A kindergarten is able to provide this, especially when beginning and second term groups are combined. Those older children stimulate with new ideas, and those younger, help to make them feel a little more important, which is often helpful to timid quiet children. Play is a natural part of the life of the five year old, and should comprise a large portion of the daily kindergarten program. With suitable materials and guidance, it can be a most constructive part as it builds bodies, minds, language, imagination, social awareness, and provides a release for feelings and tensions.

The Value of Play

An active child at play is using many muscles, even while playing indoors. Outdoor play has the added advantage of sunshine, fresh air, and the chance for more vigorous activities. Whether in or out, the child at play is developing physically and building a strong body. As he builds with blocks, looks at books, works a puzzle, he is building a strong mind. His communication with other children and the teacher helps him in his language development. Creative toys and dramatic play in which children engage builds their imagination. The sharing, planning, working and playing with others builds social awareness. Play is an all around builder of the whole child.

Probably more than any other kindergarten activity, play gives the child valuable experiences in social attitudes. As he learns to share toys and materials, take turns, and consider the wishes of the group, he is actually living in a miniature society and developing attitudes toward it. When a child builds a fire engine out of blocks, delivers milk to the doll corner, buys groceries at the kindergarten store, or busies himself in other dramatic play, he is engaging in activities which lay the foundations for future experiences in the social studies field. The wise teacher makes good use of the play period, by noticing the various areas of interest which arise, and helping children to develop additional worthwhile ones. Teachers realize that the same center of interest does not appeal to everyone in the class, and it might be only a small group which originates an idea, but he is alert to evaluate important child-initiated activities and to promote those which have worthwhile learning possibilities and which might interest a larger number of children. The teacher, for example, might bring out the inside cardboard from a roll of paper, or some similar item, for the firemen to use as a hose, and through discussion later, stimulate the desire to go outside to find the nearest fire hydrant, in order to learn where the fireman gets water for the hose. In such a manner the child learns the meaning of new words and concepts and builds a strong background for reading, social studies, and other subjects in the years to come. (A further discussion of social studies will be found in the chapter on "Social Understandings and Development."

The teacher should set the stage, so to speak, by providing toys and materials which will stimulate worthwhile play, and arranging for trips and other learning experiences which may later be relived in dramatic play. From observation of children, the teacher can get many leads: the books they might be interested in, the trips which they might take, and salvage materials he might obtain to enrich their play further. Play is natural for the child. Learning which takes place during play is retained, for it becomes an integrated part of the child.

Through observation and listening, the teacher can learn a great deal about his children, which will help his management of them. He will notice the immature ones, those who stay on the fringe, those who are leaders, those who are timid and shy, those who are not afraid to explore, and those who feel left out of things. He will have to know, when to step in and help and when not to. Though children need to be with others they also need times when they can be alone, perhaps to think, to investigate, to experiment, or just to be away from others.

Play provides a chance for the child to grow at his own individual rate. Growing cannot be rushed nor forced. Some children in kindergarten are not ready for all of the experiences for which the majority are ready and which are provided in a modern kindergarten. Some might not be ready to sit quietly with a group, or to listen to a complete story, to join in a game. It is no fault of theirs nor anyone else, but merely that they have not grown enough in a particular area. In play they can enter into the activity they are ready for, and develop at their own rate.

Play also provides opportunity for the child to express his feelings and find a release for tensions. The teacher cannot allow a child to hurt others, knock down their blocks, nor run in the room just because he feels like it, but he can understand why the child wants to do those things, accept him but not his actions, and be a better teacher because of this understanding. Rather than blame the child for the way he feels, the teacher can discuss the situation frankly with him, make him realize as a teacher he understands why he feels the way he does but make it clear that he cannot express these feelings in ways which hurt others. The teacher too, like everyone else, has feelings which pile up inside him, but the mature adult knows safe ways for releasing these feelings without hurting others. Children need to develop ways to do this also. In the work period, they find ways with crayons, paint, finger paint, clay and other materials; in the play period, with dolls, and other toys. The kindergarten teacher plays a most important role in developing good mental health among the children. A chapter further along describes the social development in kindergarten.

Indoor Play Materials

Most kindergartens have available for play time wooden puzzles, matching games, books, a sand box, large blocks, small blocks with pegs, trucks, trains, cars, doll corner furnishings, such as beds, table, cupboard, dishes, stove, sink, refrigerator, and other toys which interest a five year old. If not, the teacher might first discuss the needs with his principal to see if these items might be ordered, if not he could try to obtain them from friends whose children no longer use these kinds of toys, seek the help of the parents in collecting as many items as possible, or make many of them himself.

Shelves for toys. Orange crates, apple boxes, or strong cardboard cartons obtained from large grocery stores may be painted attractive colors, and used to store toys.

Stove. A stove may be made of one apple box, turned on its side, with the solid ends of an orange crate used for legs. Burners may be painted on the top with metallic or black paint.

Sink. This can be made in the same way, with a hole cut in the top, just the size for a square dishpan to be inserted.

Cupboard. A cupboard for dishes may be made of an orange crate standing on end, painted and fixed with cloth curtains.

Matching Games. These may be made by using two identical picture books, and mounting one set of pictures on a large cardboard, (about eight by ten inches), and the other on small individual cards, (for the matching cards). Flower seed catalogues, bird books, stars or other gummed stickers for number games are also possibilities.

Felt pieces. Felt pieces, and colored paper backed with sandpaper, cut into various shapes may be kept in a cigar box for the children to use on the felt board.

Color game. A color game may be made with only cardboard, a paper fastener, two bottle caps or big buttons, and crayons. A winding path is drawn on a large cardboard and divided into several small sections, each one of which is colored one of eight colors, red, yellow, blue, orange, green, purple, brown, or black. A spinner is made by mounting a cardboard arrow, by means of a paper fastener, over a circle divided into eight wedges, one for every color. When the arrow is spun, whichever color it points to is the color to which the child moves his bottle cap on the path of colors.

Store. Shelves for a store may be made of blocks, or two or three strong boxes, and a table used for a counter. Small cans and boxes are used to stock the shelves.

Bean bags. Sturdy material, such as denim or canvas can be used for making bean bags of various shapes and colors.

Puppets. Puppets can be made of socks (with eyes, nose, and mouth of felt), of wooden spoons (with cotton wrapped around the spoon part and covered with nylon hose for the head, and dressed), or of papier-mâché or asbestos (wrapped around a cardboard roll large enough for the middle finger) and also dressed with scrap material.

Puppet stage. A puppet stage, which can also double as a television screen has already been described in the chapter on language and literature.

Water play. Children enjoy the feeling of water, and once they have learned to follow directions can usually be depended upon to use it carefully during play time. Small orange juice cans, half filled with water, and paint brushes can be provided for children to use on the blackboard. Some special day they might wash doll dishes or doll clothes or even some of the doll furniture. They also enjoy washing the tables after work time or just before a party. On clear warm days cans of water and brushes can be taken out of doors and used for outside painting.

Wood work. With a few hammers and nails and scrap wood from a lumber company or house under construction, children can make many articles, but definite rules must be set up for their safety. A work bench with a vise or C-clamp, and saws add to the enjoyment but are not absolutely necessary. The same paints used for painting pictures may be used for wood, with the advantages of easy clean-up and fast drying.

Dress up clothes. Clean skirts, blouses, dresses, men's shirts, badges, ties, purses all add to the fun of make believe in kindergarten.

Street and traffic light. Tagboard can be used for the edges of a street, and a simple traffic light made of a box and colored paper, with red lights on two opposing sides and green lights on the others, so the children can turn the box to change the signals.

Safety boy belts. If real belts are not available from the safety patrol, the teacher can make them of sturdy material, leaving the ends which go around the waist open so they will fit any child.

Articles for the sand table. Many cast-off kitchen utensils will find good use here, such as measuring cups, sieves, tea strainers, funnels, pans, pie pans, and so forth.

Other items. Many discarded articles can enrich a play experience: scarves, bed-spreads, curtains, cigar boxes, pieces of net, a steering wheel, and tickets are a few possibilities.

Outdoor Play and Living

Ordinarily not much equipment is provided for outdoor use, though outdoor play, when the weather permits, is most important from a health standpoint. Not every kindergarten has a private play area adjoining the room, but most schools have playgrounds for the gym classes, and the kindergarten teacher can probably make arrangements to use one corner sometime during the morning and afternoon. Even if it is necessary to carry toys quite a distance, children do not mind. If each carries one or two, many of the toys used in indoor play can be taken out, if such outdoor use will not harm them. Large blocks, doll buggies, certain unbreakable dolls, trucks, cars, trains, hoops, balls, old books, and ring toss games are possibilities. Several homemade or inexpensive articles, reserved expressly for outdoor play may be included also.

Ideally the kindergarten would have its private play yard equipped with permanent equipment such as swings, slides, large pipes, jungle gym, and other items to climb on and through. A cement walk around the yard makes an ideal road for wagons and tricycles when the children play train, boat, or truck. Locked outdoor storage space is helpful.

Homemade stilts. With a juice can opener, make two holes in the unopened end of a large can, near the edge, exactly opposite each other. Put a rope about forty inches long through the holes and tie on inside of can. Cans should be large enough for children to stand on them, holding ropes in their hands, and lifting each one as the corresponding foot is lifted.

Ropes. Ropes can be cut into four or five foot lengths and used for jump ropes or horse reins. Children need to be reminded that they must never be put around anyone's neck, nor used to tie someone up.

Flying saucers. Plastic discs may be bought or cardboard discs may be made by the teacher and colored by the children in spiral designs for throwing out of doors. Children learn a lot about air currents by sailing these discs. Plastic tops from coffee cans are excellent.

Large cartons. Cartons may be used in many ways for cars, boats or trains, stoves, refrigerators, or cupboards (in an outdoor doll corner,) or for shelves for a store. The problem becomes that of storage, but if various sizes are used, several may be nested together, one inside another.

Digging tools. If a small section of ground can be used for digging, or for a garden, the teacher will be most fortunate. Large spoons, hand trowels, and sturdy shovels are good for digging and bring the child in close touch with the earth. Though children may start out to make a garden, their discovery of bugs, earth worms, beetles, ants, and other insects is a worthwhile by-product. Radishes are easily grown, and germinate so quickly that children derive a lot out of the experience of preparing the soil, planting the seeds, caring for them, and seeing the radishes develop. A radish party with bread and butter sandwiches provides a happy climax for the effort. Flowers which bloom in the fall and grow easily without too much care, such as zinnias, cleome, and marigolds, might be planted in order to have flowers during the period school is in session. Spring blooming bulbs may be planted as part of the school landscaping.

Water play. In very warm weather a large tub or dishpan, half filled with water, can be used for sailing boats, or experiments with objects which float or sink. Such activities need to be very closely supervised.

Soap bubbles. Individual paper cups with a small amount of soap powder, and water, and a straw in each are fine for blowing bubbles on a warm day, when it does not matter if a little water is spilled. This should be a treat, however, not part of the every day outdoor play.

Carriers. Cartons, or bushel baskets with cloth wrapped around the handles, may be used for carrying toys in and out, and if marked with pictures, the child may easily find the proper place to put his toy when through playing with it.

Signal. A bell or whistle should be used to get the attention of the children if the group is large, especially in case of an emergency. Special signals may be taught: one long whistle note - "stand still right where you are"; two whistle notes - "come here".

Wheeled toys. If cement or black top play space is available, wheeled toys such as wagons and tricycles can be used, on take-a-turn basis, and will provide exercise for the leg muscles particularly.

Outdoor living need not be limited to the play period alone. Children enjoy having other activities outside as well. If paper is clipped to a large piece of cardboard with a paper clip, and cans of crayons are placed around the yard children may draw outside. Story time, singing time, rhythm period (with a drum for accompaniment,) and game time can all be successfully handled out of doors, and add much to their enjoyment. If a private play yard is not provided, the teacher will need to use his ingenuity to find an appropriate spot. He should remember to notify the office, however, if such a spot is not close at hand. Children must not be taken across any street without the approval of the principal and the written permission of the parent, in most school systems.

Chapter XI

Game Time in Kindergarten

Games are like stories, in that one never gets tired of old favorites. Children love a variety, however, and teachers need to know many. There will be times when the teacher will want an active one, other times, when he will want a quiet one. Whatever the game, however, he should keep in mind that every child should participate, and select the game accordingly. There are many fine games, such as "Doggie, Your Bone is Gone", or "Color Dodge", which permit only two children at a time to have turns. With a large class, it would take so long to give everyone a turn, that such a game would not be a wise choice, especially at the beginning of the term. Later on, when children have learned to listen and follow directions, the teacher might teach such a game to the class as a whole. Then, when he feels they understand how to play it, he might divide them into two groups, choosing a child to be "the teacher" for each one, and supervising both groups at once. At the beginning of the term, however, singing games and games in which many have turns at a time, will be more successful.

Each teacher should know some basic games, (that is games which can be changed according to the season), ball games, color games, musical games, thought games, singing games, and outdoor games. As a general rule children can do their own choosing of those to have the next turns if taught how to do this at the beginning. It must be emphasized that each child chooses only one child to take his place, and he must be someone who has not already had a turn. In every game, the teacher should be alert to possibilities of making use of speech, counting, thinking or problem solving in order to make the experience as rich as possible.

Basic Games

"Old Mother Puss." Children sit on chairs in a circle. In the middle is a chair for Old Mother Puss, around whom are six to ten pussies, (or as many as necessary to give everyone a turn in three sessions of the game that day.) Together the children say this verse:

> "Old Mother Puss lies fast asleep.
> Her babies, too, make not a peep.
> But little pussies like to play,
> So they softly creep away."

Babies hide, but only one in a hiding place, while Mother Puss keeps eyes closed and hands in lap. When all have found a hiding place, they say,

"Old Mother Puss wakes up to see
No baby pussies. Where can they be?
Softly she calls, 'Meow.'"

Babies must answer once each time the Mother Puss "meows", until they are found. As Mother Puss finds a pussy, she says, "I found you, Jean", and Jean then returns to the floor close to Mother Puss' chair. Before all are found, Mother Puss counts the pussies around her chair to see how many are still hiding. Speech, rhyme, counting, listening, sound direction are involved. (Variations might include owls and baby owls saying "Oooooh. Oooooh," Turkeys saying "Gobble, gobble", reindeer pawing ground, rabbits thumping feet, for Halloween, Thanksgiving, Christmas, and Easter, respectively, and children will delight in being asked to think up ways of changing the game).

"Huckle Buckle Beanstalk." Children may be seated on chairs in a circle, while eight or ten hide their eyes at the blackboard, and one child hides a bell, (or any object which makes noise) some place where it can be seen as one walks by. He rings the bell where he is about to put it, returns to his chair and says, "Ready." The children who have been covering their eyes then look for the bell, but when they see it, they do not touch it, nor say anything, but return to their chairs and say "Huckle, Buckle, Beanstalk." The one who has hidden it watches to see who finds it first, and when all have finally found it, announces, "Jimmy found it first so he may hide it." Listening, sound direction, and speech are all involved in this game.

"Hunting and Finding." About forty pumpkins may be cut out of orange colored paper for children to hide. Boys may be asked first to close their eyes, while the girls line up in front of the teacher to receive three or four pumpkins each to hide, hiding each pumpkin in a different place, and where it can be seen when one walks by. When all pumpkins have been hidden, the teacher says "Ready," and the boys start to look for them, each one finding as many as he can, but without running. The teacher asks the girls if there are any pumpkins the boys still have not found, and if not, tells the boys to return to their places to count theirs. The teacher then asks for those who found only one to bring it up, then two, and so on, asking the group to count with him as they are dropped into a box, or asking the child to count his own, depending on the size and maturity of the group. There should be enough pumpkins that every one may find some. This involves mainly counting, but observation and speech are also included. Then the procedure is reversed, with the boys hiding the pumpkins and the girls looking for them.

"Dog and Bone." Children may be seated on chairs in a circle, with one child, who is the "dog" on a chair in the middle with his eyes closed and hands in his lap, and a bone under the chair. Another child is chosen to take the bone away and hide it under him. When this has been done, all softly say "Doggie, your bone is gone." The "dog" has three chances to guess correctly. If he does so on the first, second, or third guess he is given another turn to be the "dog." If he does not guess correctly in three chances, he asks, "Who has my bone?" and the child who has the bone becomes the new "dog." Speech, counting, and listening are involved. (Variations might include a witch and broomstick for

Halloween, turkey and corn for Thanksgiving, chicken and eggs for Easter, and so forth.)

"Pumpkin Scramble." Children may be seated on chairs in a circle. About a third of the group may be chosen at one time to stand in the center ready to scramble for the paper pumpkins which the teacher tosses into the air, a few at a time. When all have been gathered up, the children return to their chairs to count them, and then, as the teacher calls the number, the child brings his pumpkins to him, either counting them himself as he drops them into a box, or if the group is large, just giving them to the teacher until the end, when those of the winner are counted by the whole group.

Ball Games

"Hot Ball." Children are seated on the floor in a circle. They pretend the big ball is a ball of fire which they must push away, not catch and hold. No one is allowed to reach for a ball, but must wait patiently until the ball comes to him. When children understand this rule, more balls may be added one at a time. They must be taught to stop the game when the teacher says, "Hold the balls."

"Hit the Big Ball." Children are seated as for hot ball. A big ball is placed in the middle of the circle, and this ball is never to be rolled. Children have four or five smaller balls which they roll to try to hit the big one. If a ball stops in the middle, no one may get it, but it must be knocked back into play by another ball.

"White Elephant." Children may be seated on chairs in a circle, or on the floor. One child bounces the ball in front of five children, counting each child as he does so. These five children go to the center of the circle and the others roll the ball toward them. If a child in the center is hit, he must sit down. The game continues until there is only one left in the middle, the winner, who then starts the game all over again by choosing five more. Another version of this game is that the one who chooses the five, bounces the ball once more as the signal that the game is going to start and then tries to tag the children with the ball. Motor coordination and counting are included.

"Ball and Hoop." Children may be seated on the floor in a circle, in the middle of which a hoop is placed. Five or six small balls are used and children try to get the balls into the hoop. Score may be kept on the blackboard by a girl scorkeeper and a boy scorekeeper

"Basketball." This is played like "Ball and Hoop" except that only one ball is used and an empty waste paper basket is in the middle instead of a hoop.

"Mum Ball." Children may be seated on chairs in a circle, and a ball rolled back and forth. One person who is "it" is the only one allowed to talk. He tries to make others talk and the first one who does, becomes "it" and has to do likewise.

Color Games

The games that follow may be considered basic games, for the colored paper which is used may be cut in any shape, depending upon the season.

"Color Dodge." Children are seated on chairs in a circle, and one is chosen to cover his eyes at the blackboard, while another chooses one of the eight common colors to be pinned to his back, (or, if fixed with string, to be hung around his neck). When the child with the color on his back says, "Ready," the one who has been covering his eyes tries to see what color it is. When he does, he calls out the name of the color and the game proceeds after each of the two children chooses a new person to take his place. Some teachers choose three or four to cover their eyes, while three or four have colors on their backs, in order to give more children turns at the same time.

"Reds Change Places." The children should be seated on chairs in a circle, and each one given a color. The teacher says, "Reds stand up." When all the reds are standing and see where the other reds are, they are told, "Reds, change places." Those with red must then find a different chair to sit on as they must not sit on their own chairs again. When every color has had a chance to change, the children may trade colors, so they each have a different one next time. After children have played the game several times a chair might be placed in the middle and when they are told to change places, the first one to sit on the chair in the middle gets to call the next color. Color discrimination and the fact that all take part are the advantages of this game.

"I Spy Something Red." Children may be seated on chairs in a circle and told to close their eyes while one child whispers to the teacher the object he chooses of a certain color. When he says, "Ready," they open their eyes and he says, "I spy something red." Children notice the red objects in the room and try to guess which one he means. The one who guesses correctly is allowed to choose the next color.

"I Spy." Children are seated in a circle on chairs. One child stands in the middle and the following is said by the child and the group.

Child:	"I spy."
Group:	"Whom do you spy?"
Child:	"A little girl?"
Group:	"What is her name?"
Child:	"She has no name."
Group:	"What is her color?"
Child:	"She has a pink dress, pink socks, black shoes and a white bow in her hair."

The child thus described then comes to the center, and each hops on one foot, trying to make the other put his foot down first. The child who hops the longest gets the next turn to say, "I spy." Children should have hands on their hips while hopping. Speech, color, and motor coordination are involved.

"What Is Missing?" All the children who have not had a turn in another game might be asked to look at all the colors arranged on a table, and then cover their eyes while one color is taken away. Colors can then be re-arranged and the children open their eyes to see which color is missing.

Sound Games

"Hello, Mr. Bear." Children are seated in a circle on chairs and one child who has his eyes covered is on one of two chairs in the middle. The teacher points to a child to go to the other chair in the middle and say, "Hello, Mr. Bear." Mr. Bear tries to guess whose voice it is, but if he cannot, he may ask a question, such as, "What did you have for breakfast?", "How old are you?", or "What color are your clothes?" Mr. Bear may have another turn if he guesses correctly, or the other child may become "Mr. Bear" if he does not. This involves speech, listening, and color discrimination.

"What is That Noise?" Children may be seated in a circle on chairs, and asked to cover their eyes while one child makes a noise with something, such as sweeping the floor with a broom, pushing a squeaky doll buggy, dropping pegs, beating a drum. When the child returns to his chair and says "Ready," the others guess what the noise was. The first to guess correctly makes the next noise.

"Follow the Sound." Children may be seated in a circle on chairs, while five or six cover their eyes at the blackboard. One child hides an object, returns to his place and says, "Ready." The children at the blackboard hold hands as they go together to look for the hidden object, guided by the teacher playing the piano loudly, when they are near it, and softly when they are not. The first one to find the object, hides it the next time.

Musical Games

"Magic Carpet." Children should be seated in a group while the game is explained and then all stand to take part. Newspapers, representing carpets, are placed here and there on the floor. The children are to walk on the carpets while the music plays but when the music stops, anyone on a magic carpet is out of the game. Motor coordination and music are involved, and everyone is included in such a game.

"Stoop Tag." Children skip, walk, or run while the music is played, but when it stops, they are to get into a stooping position. The last one to do so is out of the game. Music and motor coordination are involved, and again, it is possible for everyone to take part.

"Come Along." Children should be standing in circle formation. One child skips around and grasps the hand of some one from the circle who then skips with him, in turn grasping a new one right away, who also skips with the others, all holding hands. The choosing and skipping continues until the music stops, at which time all run back to their original places in the circle. The first one back starts the game again.

It is well to limit the number of children skipping to five or six.

"Musical Ball." Children should be seated on chairs in a circle. A ball is passed around the circle from one to the other, while the music plays. When the music stops, those who are touching the ball must sit on the floor in the center. When several have been sent to the center they may return to the circle and the game started over again. Everyone may take part, and music, and motor coordination are involved. Counting may also be included if the teacher desires to limit the number of children who go to the center.

"Bridges." Children should stand in a circle while two children join hands to form a bridge. When the music plays, the children march around the circle passing under the bridge. When the music stops, the child caught under the bridge must sit in the center of the circle, until another child is caught, at which time he joins him to form another bridge on the circle. The game may be stopped at any time, or continued until there is only one child left, the winner.

Thought Games

Such games have already been referred to in the chapter concerning language and literature, but are included here again for easy reference.

Simple questions or riddles, based on previous group experiences, such as "Name five vegetables." "What nursery rhyme is about an egg?", or "I went into Mr. McGregor's garden. Who am I?" can be printed on small pieces of colored paper and a child chosen to draw each question, to be asked of the group as a whole, or three or four contestants. Questions involving counting may also be used.

Objects mentioned in nursery rhymes, (such as a pail, clothespin, candlestick, eggshell, garden tool, crooked stick, pipe, bone, spider, three bags.) may be placed on a table and a child chosen to pick out an object and say the verse.

Asking the group to think of words which rhyme, or words which mean the opposite of certain ones, (such as big-little, dirty-clean, old-new, hot-cold, good-bad, front-back, under-over, top-bottom, sad-happy) or to think of all the round things in the room, all the things that go on wheels, or all the things in their homes which run by electricity are possibilities.

One child may be asked to think of something in the room. Others may ask twenty yes-or-no questions in trying to guess what it is.

A panel of four or five children may be asked to discuss such questions as "What would you do if you lost your mother in a downtown store?" or "What would you do if your friend got locked inside a trunk?" or "What was the funniest thing that ever happened to you? The saddest? The most frightening?" or "Why should children not play with matches?" or "What would you do if a stranger offered you a ride?" or "What is your favorite story? Poem? Song? Kindergarten activity?"

Singing Games

Because most kindergarten teachers are already familiar with several singing games, or can find them in the music books available in most kindergartens, (complete with words, music, and directions), only a sample list of possible ones will be included here.

"Farmer in the Dell."
"Did You Ever See a Lassie?"
"London Bridge is Falling Down"
"Bluebird, Bluebird"
"Now We Dance Looby Loo"
"Skip to My Loo"
"Fair Rosie"
"My Pigeon House"
"A rig-a-gig-gig"
"Five Little Chicadees"

Many of the above games originated in England and might require an explanation or change in order to be most meaningful to American children. However, American children enjoy them, whether changed or not.

Outdoor Games

"Mr. Fox." One child is chosen to be "Mr. Fox," and stands about twenty yards away from the others who are in a line, shoulder to shoulder, holding hands. The children say, "What time is it, Mr. Fox?" and "Mr. Fox" responds with any time he likes. If he says, "One o'clock," the children take one step together, stop in a straight line as before, and ask again, "What time is it, Mr. Fox?". If he says, "Three o'clock," they take three steps and so on, but if he says "Twelve o'clock, midnight!" that is the signal that he is going to chase them, and the children try to get back to the starting point without being caught. Children who are caught become "Mr. Fox's" helpers, but only "Mr. Fox" calls out the time. Vigorous exercise, counting, and speech are involved, and all are able to participate.

"Flowers and the Wind." Some children line up shoulder to shoulder to be the wind, while the rest decide on the name of one flower, which they are supposed to be. One of the members of the flower group is asked to choose one at a time of the wind group to guess the name of the flower. If the guess is incorrect, the "flowers" say, "No, we are not_____." If the guess is correct, they try to run back to the starting point without being caught. Those caught go on the wind side, and the game proceeds. The game may be varied by using names of vegetables, fruits, familiar tools, colors, wild animals, tame animals, or items from other classifications. The necessary vocabulary and concepts must be developed before the game can be played. Vigorous activity, balanced with quiet listening are also involved, and everyone may be included.

"Run for Your Supper." Children stand in circle formation while one child walks around it and then places a ball between two of the children in the formation, telling them, "Run for your supper." They go around the circle and the first one back to the ball is the winner to start the game again. He may tell them to skip, hop, jump, or walk to add variety.

"Chinese Wall." An area about six feet wide is designated as the wall, and one child is chosen to be on the wall. The others form two lines, shoulder to shoulder on each side of the wall, about thirty feet from it. When the child on the wall shouts, "Run!" the children try to cross the wall and get to the other side without being caught. A player may be caught only when he is on the wall. Those caught must stay on the wall to help catch others. It is an active game in which all may participate, making it a very good game to play in cold weather.

"Races." Girls form a line, shoulder to shoulder, about thirty feet from the boys who hold their hands out ready to be tagged. The teacher designates how the girls are to race up to the boys and back, (running, skipping, jumping on two feet, hopping, and so forth), and then says, "On your mark. Get set. Go." Girls race up to boys, tag any boy's hand, and race back to place. The first one back is the winner. This is then reversed with the boys forming a line and the girls doing the running.

"Cat and Mouse." Children hold hands in circle formation. One child is chosen to be the cat who stands outside of the circle, and another to be the mouse on the inside of the circle. The "cat" asks the "mouse" first if he is ready, and if so, chases the mouse in and out of the circle, while the children try to help the mouse, by letting him in or out of the circle, but not the cat. Once the children understand the game, the class may be divided into two or three groups so everyone may have a turn in a shorter period of time.

Chapter XII

Science

Five year olds are so curious about things and so eager to understand more about them that science is most fascinating in kindergarten. Nature, which is very close to the child's world, offers a never ending source of delight. Physics and chemistry also have their beginnings here in the kindergarten. Experiments, demonstrations, collections, and various projects all have a place in kindergarten, if kept on a level which the child can understand.

The teacher need not be a science major for he can easily obtain information from the science teacher, encyclopedias, elementary textbooks or other reference books. He need not feel insecure nor embarrassed when he must say, "I do not know, but let's find out." The beginning teacher will find there will be many times when he will be stumped by the questions of a five year old and not just in science! He will enjoy increasing his own scientific knowledge right along with the children as he makes use of available reference and children's books. There will be many phases of nature, formerly passed by without notice and now discovered which the teacher too will find fascinating. His life will be enriched because of them.

The kindergarten teacher has a wonderful opportunity to help the child develop correct concepts, enlarge his vocabulary, and give him a good background for material he will read in later years. The more information the kindergarten teacher has, the richer can be the experiences he provides for his children, but he should remember that children need time to experiment and to discover things for themselves, and not be dished out factual information. Science instruction might well come out of the group's particular interests. Some suggestions for possible activities which provide first-hand experiences follow.

Observation of Nature

In the fall. In communities where there are few gardens from which children may get flowers to bring to school, the teacher may be able to bring an occasional bunch, just so children may enjoy them and learn the names of some of the most common, such as rose, zinnia, chrysanthemum, and aster. Walks may be taken to notice points of natural interest in the particular neighborhood.

There may be apple or thornapple trees to see, acorns or other seeds to gather, grasshoppers to catch or weeds to collect, and bring back to kindergarten. A pint mason jar, with a screen top, and the outer ring of a lid, can be used to put one or two grasshoppers in, but if the teacher has a larger container, such as a cut down gallon jug, she can prepare a better home for them from which children can observe their activities. When grasshoppers or any other wild live animals are brought to the classroom, they should be kept only a day or two and then returned to a habitat similar to the one in which they were found. Tall grass and water should be provided in the classroom.

Crocuses or tulips might be planted in an outdoor garden if there is space in which to do so, but if not, narcissus bulbs can be grown in pots indoors. Leaves of brilliant color may be collected, usually in late October when they change color, and pressed between wax paper under blocks to make them stay flat, or just arranged on a shelf to be replaced in a day or two as they become withered and dry.

As changes take place in the fall as plant and animal life prepare for winter, the teacher should call these to the attention of the children. Concepts which the adult takes for granted are new to the child. The child's discovery of them is a big thrill to him. Even the common dandelion provides an exciting experience in science when the child himself pulls apart a white-haired dandelion and discovers the seeds, and learns how they travel on animals, people and in the wind. Spiders spinning their webs, birds and butterflies migrating, squirrels storing food for winter, days getting shorter, turtles hibernating, are other possibilities A cocoon on its twig may be brought back to be kept in the kindergarten in a screen container.

In the winter. Snowsuit-and-boot weather in certain parts of the country makes it difficult to take walks in the middle of the kindergarten session because of the length of time it takes to dress and undress, but the teacher might get the children ready earlier on some days to take walks to notice such things as a squirrel's nest (which looks like a bunch of leaves high in a tree), evergreen trees, other trees and bushes which have lost all their leaves, or animal tracks in the snow.

Winter in some sections of the country provides a fine opportunity to explore the concepts of melting and freezing. After the first snowfall, children may bring a little snow into the room and place it on a dish for all to observe, thus developing the concept of "melting." On cold days, water may be placed in a dish outside on the window sill until it freezes into ice. A simple weather chart, such as one with colors and symbols to designate various kinds of weather may also be maintained. Fish, turtles, and other pets and plants may be cared for indoors and experiments such as those suggested later on can be conducted during this period when children must spend a great deal of time indoors.

In the spring. Anticipating that the children will enjoy giving plants to their mothers for Mother's Day, the teacher may have the children plant nasturtiums or other flowers with large seeds in a flat, paper cup, egg shell, or milk carton cut lengthwise. Petunias often are successful, but the seeds being very tiny are difficult for children to handle.

Forsythia branches, and those from fruit trees when they first start to bud, may be brought indoors early in the spring and, if placed in water, will open in about a week. Pussywillow branches will develop roots and go to seed if placed in water thus showing how some new plants can be developed from cuttings. Some pussywillows may be preserved as they are, if placed in a vase without water.

Yarn, string, cloth, and raffia may be placed outside for the use of robins in building their nests. Children may want to try building a nest like a robin's nest, in order to appreciate what a difficult job the bird does. Walks may be taken with the express purpose of looking for robins, nests, cabbage butterflies, buds on bushes and trees, and later, new leaves, fruit trees in blossom, and insects. An oriole's nest would be a particularly interesting find to watch the year around.

Later in the spring grass may be planted in a small dish, a pine cone, or better yet, in the school lawn where needed. Bugs and worms are likely to be found while digging out of doors. Seeds of flowers which will bloom in the fall, when children will again be back in school, may be planted in an outdoor garden. Zinnias, asters, nasturtiums, "ragged sailors", and marigolds need little care and are likely to weather the hot summer unattended. Radish seeds germinate quickly and are ready to eat in about twenty days. Thus children can plant and harvest a crop of radishes before school is out in the spring.

The teacher or a child might be able to bring in tadpoles for the children to care for and observe as they change into frogs, but if not, no doubt there will be some in the science room which the kindergarten teacher might borrow or share. Some museums, zoos, and school districts have animal lending libraries where a teacher may borrow an animal such as a rabbit, mouse, or chicken for a day or two, thus providing an opportunity for the class to observe various animals without the teacher having to assume permanent care for them. The principal or science teacher can usually provide the necessary information about such a service.

The teacher who is not fortunate enough to have an appropriate place for digging can at least make use of other phenomena of nature such as the sky, clouds, moon, sun, shadows, wind, lightning and thunder.

It is essential to prepare the children ahead of time for trips or walks of any type in order that they may understand what they are looking for and what they hope to find out as a result of this experience. Upon returning to the classroom from the trip there should be time allowed for a short discussion of all the things that the children have seen and learned. The teacher will want to establish definite rules for the children to observe while taking walks and trips as he is responsible for their safety. Children must understand that no one may leave the group, that they must stay close together but without crowding, that they must walk on the sidewalk, not the grass, and that they must let the teacher lead. Though he walks in front, the teacher must keep his eyes on the group, and every time they turn a corner he should stop to make sure all have followed. It should not be necessary for children to walk in lines except perhaps at the beginning of the term until the teacher feels he can depend upon them to follow directions. A "buddy" system helps to keep track of all and can be used very effectively. It is a good safety practice to take a whistle along in order to signal the children, and to establish a few specific signals consistent with playground signals. For instance, two whistle notes mean they should come close to the teacher and listen. If there is a driveway to cross, one whistle note will get their attention first, and remind them to stop, look, and await the teacher's signal that it is safe to cross, walking close together and watching while crossing. Before re-entering the school, everyone should become quiet and recognize that the trip is over and they are back in school. It is helpful to establish the system that the first boy holds the door open for all to pass through, both in leaving and re-entering the building.

When collecting live specimens while doing gardening or taking trips, if the teacher feels at all squeamish about handling worms, or bugs, he should be careful that he does not impart this feeling to the children. It is a known fact that children are not afraid of even snakes, but rather that adults have projected their fears to them. If a teacher is reluctant to handle certain animals the problem can best be resolved by taking appropriate containers on each trip.

Projects for Kindergarten

In addition to maintaining a weather chart, which has already been discussed, there are many other projects which might be carried on, such as building an aquarium, an indoor garden, maintaining a bird feeding station in winter, caring for plants in the classroom, watching a sweet potato or carrot plant develop, or observing a thermometer or barometer from day to day. Suggestions for carrying on these projects will help both the beginning and experienced teacher, who gradually will be able to have more and more of them going on in his classroom.

Maintaining an aquarium. One of the first science undertakings might be that of building an aquarium. Once completed this is an activity that can be continued throughout the school year. The bottom of the aquarium should be covered with about one or more inches of sand or aquarium gravel, which has been washed clean by running water through it until it is clear. If water plants and snails are kept in the aquarium, it should not be necessary to change the water as they will eat up the refuse. They would also enjoy an occasional snack of lettuce. The water plants will give off oxygen which the fish need, and the fish will give off carbon dioxide which is needed by the plants, thus making a good balance if the correct number of each can be worked out. Rocks or marbles rather than shells should be placed around the plants to anchor them into the sand as fish are likely to scratch themselves on shells. The water should stand several days before the fish are added in order that it become room temperature and also because water directly from the tap sometimes contains too much chlorine for fish. Letting it stand gives the chlorine a chance to escape. New water will have to be added from time to time to replace that which evaporates. The aquarium should be kept in a light place, but out of direct sunlight.

Fish should be fed only two or three times a week, and uneaten food should be removed by means of a dip tube. Goldfish are probably the easiest to raise but guppies and zebra fish can be kept if the room does not get too cold over winter weekends. Catfish help keep a tropical fish aquarium clean and are fun to watch.

A glass top or piece of saran wrap will help keep dust out and decrease evaporation. If it should become necessary to change the water, it may be siphoned out into a pail placed lower than the aquarium by filling a rubber tube full of water, holding both ends closed until one end is held in the aquarium and other lower, in a pail. The water will then flow through the tube into the pail.

Caring for something such as an aquarium is a more educational experience for children than observing one. They should participate in experiences such as siphoning out water.

Caring for a turtle. A home may be made for a turtle by having gravel or rocks built up higher than the water on one side of a flat shallow pan so that the turtle may go into the water or on the rocks as he chooses. About one and a half inches of water is enough, just so the turtle can swallow his food under water. In order to keep the turtles confined, this pan should be placed in a large cardboard or wooden box. There are some turtles, however, which do not need water. Worms or ground beef may be fed to them, in addition to the regular turtle food which can be purchased at a pet or ten cent store. If the food is tied on a string, children can see the mouths of the turtles open as they grab for food.

Developing a sweet potato plant. An ordinary sweet potato may be placed in a jar so that only half of it is submerged in water, and in a few weeks it will start to show roots on the bottom and green stems will sprout from the upper part, developing into a lovely vine which is very easy to care for. When the vine gets too large to care for, a leaf with the stem attached may be cut off, placed in water, and it, too, will develop roots and a vine. This is the actual way sweet potato farmers start their new plants.

If the top of a carrot is cut off and placed in a shallow dish of water, it, too, will sprout.

Planting bulbs indoors. A bowl about five inches in diameter may be filled with clean pebbles, and bulbs worked into the stones, so that the upper third of the bulbs are left uncovered. The bowl should be kept filled with water during the lifetime of the plant. For about the first three weeks, it should be placed in a cool, dark place, until the roots are well developed, and then in a lighter but cool place until ready to flower.

Children will realize the similarity of narcissus bulbs to onions and can learn that the onion is a bulb which we eat. Through other experiences, they can learn we also eat roots of certain plants (radish), leaves (spinach, lettuce), and flowers, (cauliflower, broccoli).

Planting seeds indoors. If grass, petunia, nasturium or other seeds are planted in cups or milk cartons cut lengthwise, pebbles should be put in the bottom before the dirt to provide drainage. A piece of charcoal will help prevent souring. Bean seeds grow very quickly and may be planted at various time intervals in order that children may learn the different stages of development and see all these stages at the same time. Instead of planting some of the bean seeds in dirt, the teacher might want to place them between layers of moist cotton so the children may see what happens as the seeds develop roots in the ground.

Collecting articles. A table or shelf should be available so the children may exhibit leaves, seeds, weeds, nuts, shells, insects, certain toys which they collect, in a way that makes it possible to examine them and to see how they work. Items selected for exhibit might include the inside of a music box, a wind up car, an alarm clock, or seed pods.

Providing a bird feeding station. A wooden platform attached to the outside window ledge would be the ideal arrangement for a bird feeding station for children to observe birds eating at close range. If this is not possible, a shallow cardboard box tied to the window handles will last quite a while and work satisfactorily as a feeder to lure birds close to the window for the children to observe them. Bread crumbs, sunflower seeds, chicken feed, weed seeds or commercially prepared bird seed may be used. A small tree may be used to hang popcorn, cranberries, or bread in order to make a "birds' Christmas tree."

Experiments

Children need time to discover things for themselves and to experiment. The teacher, knowing various possibilities, can set the stage and have available items which will stimulate experimentation. Sometimes he may want to have the whole group observe the same thing as they experiment with a magnet, a magnifying glass, sound, evaporation of water, things that float and things that sink. At other times, observation might be individual, as a child "studies" how a tricycle works or what happens when blocks are piled up in a crooked column. He should avoid giving the children all the information. By first finding out what they already know then presenting a situation about a certain thing, and giving them time to observe, they will arrive at their own conclusions as a result of an experiment.

With a magnet. Several items might be available for the children to try to pick up with a magnet, such as a rubber band, piece of paper, bobbie pin, little plastic car, paper clip, small piece of wood, paper fastener, nail or leaf, and children asked to guess beforehand whether a magnet will or will not pick up these items. Those which the magnet does pick up may be put into one pile and those which it does not pick up may be put into another pile.

Later paper clips might be attached to the noses of a number of colored paper fish and a fishing pole made of the magnet tied to a string. The fish can be dropped in a cardboard box and as a child catches a fish, he can say, "I caught a blue fish," or whatever color it happens to be. Numerals might be put on the fish for variation. "I caught numeral 3" a child might announce as his magnet picks up the fish with that numeral on its paper clip nose.

With water. A shallow pan of water might be placed somewhere in the room and when the water has disappeared, the children could try to figure out what has happened to it. When they have learned that the water has evaporated into the air, they might want to place one pan of water in the sun and one in the shade to see which evaporates first.

Two streaks of water might be made on the blackboard, with a sponge, one fanned and the other not, to show the effect of wind on evaporation. Water may be placed outdoors on a freezing day to turn into ice, or ice brought indoors to melt into water. It may be boiled to turn into steam, illustrating the three forms of water, depending on the temperature.

With things that float and things that sink. Children might be given a cork, a tongue depressor, a piece of paper, a nail, a marble, sponge rubber, a milk weed pod, a feather, a pencil with an eraser, a pencil without an eraser, and other items to discover which ones float and which ones sink. If these items are dropped in a large glass jar all can see what happens to each article as it is dropped in, that is, discover if it floats or sinks. The children might discuss why in either case.

With drying fruit. With a needle and thread, the teacher might make a string of grapes, having a square of paper between each one, and then place it in a spot where children can observe it daily in order to discover what happens. They might be told that it will take a long time for this thing to happen, but to watch every day until someone discovers the secret, (that they have become raisins). Plums, apricots and apples may be dried the same way or by placing them on aluminum foil paper.

With things which dissolve. Children might want to experiment with such things as sugar, salt, flour and sand, to see which dissolve and which do not. After dissolving sugar or salt in a small amount of water, it might be left for the water to evaporate and the salt or sugar crystals to appear.

Demonstrations

Sometimes experimentation is impossible or impractical for the five year old and in this case a demonstration might serve the purpose better. A teacher would not want to let the children experiment with the piano strings for example, yet watching the piano tuner at work could be a worthwhile lesson in sound. Other demonstrations such as the following are also possible:

Concerning water in the air. A foggy day might bring about a discussion concerning water in the air. Children cannot see the particles of water, but if they see water sprayed into the air by means of an atomizer they realize it can actually be there, but invisible. Children may also learn how water is sometimes taken out of the air through condensation on something cold. In winter, a can might be placed outside until it becomes very cold. If it is then brought inside and filled with water, children will see how water collects on the outside. In summer, the same demonstration may be made with ice water in a glass or paper cup.

Concerning jet propulsion. Although five year old children will not be able to grasp the concept that an action in one direction causes a corresponding action in another direction, the principle of how a jet is thrust forward may be somewhat grasped by blowing up a balloon and then letting it go as the air is expelled. A toy car may be attached to it and placed on the floor, or a paper airplane attached and held in the air for further demonstrations.

Concerning the wind. When children have learned to follow directions so they may be left on their own when the teacher is busy, the teacher might want to help them fly a kite. If the teacher does not know how to assemble one, he has only to ask an older boy. If one of the children needs help in getting the kite into the air, the older boy would again, no doubt, be very glad to help. Once it is up, the children might take turns flying it. The children should help select an area free from overhead wires and know why this is necessary for safety in kite flying.

Many museum shops sell fascinating kites from Japan. A museum expedition might include selecting and buying one.

Round circles of cardboard, about seven inches in diameter, or plastic coffee can covers, may be tossed into the air, as flying saucers, and on a windy day will sail as high as the school.

Concerning sound. Older children might be asked to demonstrate a violin, cello, string bass, or other stringed instrument in order to develop the idea that sound is caused by vibration. Children can actually see the vibrations of the bass viol string.

Glasses may be filled with varying amounts of water and tuned to the scale. Children will see how adding or pouring out some of the water affects the sound when the glass is tapped. Tapping various articles around the room will help them to become sound conscious, an important aspect of their musical development. Drums made from a variety of cans and boxes produce different tones.

Children are fascinated when they see the inside of a piano and how it works. Therefore, the teacher might open the top of the piano and let the children observe it while he plays.

Concerning astronomy. Holes may be poked in the bottom of an oatmeal box in the shape of the big dipper or other constellation. When held up so the light will shine through, it will look just like that constellation. After seeing the shape of the big dipper or other constellation the children might ask that their parents help them find it at night.

Concerning light. While the teacher is threading the film projector, he has a wonderful opportunity to show the children about light, shadows, reflected light (by a mirror or fish bowl).

Shadow puppets may be made or shadows of the children's hands and profiles may be produced on the screen.

A prism hung in a sunny window is a delight as well as a science phenomenon.

Concerning butter fat. Most kindergarten teachers like to have their children make butter, and each has his own way of doing it. An easy way is to divide a pint of whipping cream into six plastic sherbet containers, fasten the covers securely with tape, and have the class divided into six groups so each child may shake a container quickly twenty times and then pass it on to the next child. In a very short time the cream changes into whipped cream, and then finally into butter. The liquid (buttermilk) may be poured off and the butter pressed with tongue depressors to force the remaining liquid out, and then spread on crackers by the children. The children will want to sample the buttermilk as well as the butter.

Chapter XIII

Social Development and Understanding

"In kindergarten, they just learn to play together, don't they?" is a question often asked of kindergarten teachers.

People not closely associated with the five year old do not realize there is a tremendous intellectual growth as well. They do not realize that a child's play is his work. His social development is, for certain, one of the major concerns in kindergarten. His ability to get along with others, and his awareness of the society in which he lives are important aspects of his personality that need to be developed. From the small group of one's family, then the neighborhood, the child later enters a larger world, the kindergarten. Some children might have had previous experience in nursery school or Sunday School groups, but for a great majority, kindergarten is the first large group experience.

As a member of this group, he enjoys many pleasures not possible in the family or neighborhood, yet, at the same time, learns to accept his responsibilities towards others, an important part of group living. Along with this social growth, there is growth in understanding of the society in which he lives. As the kindergarten year progresses, and the children make boats, trains, fire engines, or airplanes out of blocks, and as other activities relating to the social sciences are carried out, they learn more about the bigger world about them. Their social development and understanding of society go hand in hand.

Social Development

Diversified backgrounds of children. In a public kindergarten of a large school, and in many private ones as well, the personal backgrounds of children probably will be extremely varied in regard to the size of the family, the number of children and adults in the home, the economic conditions, social status of the family, the home atmosphere, the sleeping arrangements, the availability of playmates, the culture pattern, and the religion or lack of it. Aunts, uncles and grandparents who share the home have a definite effect on the child, as does quarreling or sharing a bed with one or more brothers or sisters. An only child, who has never had anyone to play with is going to be quite different from one who has learned to share or fight with brothers, sisters and playmates.

A child who has had little or no supervision at home, or too much supervision, is likely to be quite different from the child who has had love and guidance in his pre-school years. One who feels insecure, unwanted, and frightened will contrast sharply with a child who feels secure, loved, and comfortable about himself. The kindergarten will have quite a variety of personalities, each with differing backgrounds. The more a teacher can learn of a child's background, the more he can understand the child and be a help to this child in his development.

Children will differ, too, in the experiences they have had before coming to school. Some might have visited the zoo several times, and travelled in trains, buses, and planes, while others might never have been away from their own neighborhoods. The teacher must accept each child as he comes to him, whatever his personality, background, and experiences, and, from that point in his development, guide him as far as he can in the time they are together. The teacher needs to accept the child even though he does not approve of his present conditions or actions.

The philosophy of the teacher. It is the teacher who sets the stage for the kind of social development which can take place in his room. As a teacher in a democratic society, in which human values and the importance of the individual are emphasized, (in contrast to a society where the individual is an instrument of the state), he has a responsibility to assist the child live in a democratic society. The teacher will hope to develop desirable behavior for group living, such as taking turns, sharing toys and materials, respecting the rights of others, and appreciating the contributions of others, but he will also hope to develop desirable traits in the individual, such as self-reliance, self-control, self-respect, courage, creativeness, ability to follow directions, and ability to think for one's self. He must know what goals he hopes to attain, and feel secure in his philosophy.

If the teacher believes in a very formal type of kindergarten, in which he is dictator, he will handle the activities and children in quite a different manner from the teacher who believes in a democratic kindergarten, and the importance of the individual. The latter teacher will want to provide children with as many opportunities as he possibly can to think, plan, solve problems, and express ideas. He will put emphasis on human values. He will try to have a permissive atmosphere in his room as much as possible, to encourage children to develop individually, but at the same time, he will be firm in setting certain behavioral limits. He will not want to overburden the children with rules, but will be consistent, and firm yet kind, in seeing that these limits are observed. He will realize that children have to learn to live with others, just as they learn to draw, sing, count, or anything else. He will do all in his power to help the children feel comfortable with each other, to make each one feel that he belongs, that he is needed, for the teacher knows the importance of the individual's opinion of himself in a group situation. A child who doesn't like himself will have trouble liking others and living with them.

Kindergarten as a miniature society. Kindergarten affords a fine opportunity for social development for it is a miniature society in itself, a place where children are not just learning the principles of how to live with others in the future, but are actually living in a small society of their own.

Taking turns. From the very first day, there will be occasions when the child must stand in line, to come into the building, get crayons, paper or other materials, and he will have to learn to leave a space in front of himself, not touch the other children, and not to push. The immature child may go to the front of the line each time, or the middle, and has to be reminded that they can't all get crayons at once, that others were in line first, and that he must wait his turn like the rest. There will be times when he will have to wait to play with a certain toy, to get help from the teacher, to have a turn in a game, and in many other situations. Some will learn faster than others. The teacher must be ever watchful and consistent in helping each child to develop good habits.

Sharing. In large classes, it will be necessary for children to share materials, such as crayons, scissors, paste jars, and brushes, if there are not enough to go around. Most do so very willingly. Some might be more reluctant to share a toy. There will be times when one child's desire to have a certain toy might result in conflict with another, with both children claiming to have had it first. The wise teacher might not arbitrarily decide who should keep it, but would want to talk it over with the children involved, encouraging them to think of a way to use it together, if the occasion permits. If both want the airplane, the teacher might suggest they build an airport of blocks so the airplane will have a place to land, and perhaps take turns being pilot or man in the control tower. There will be times when this is not possible, however, and the teacher will have to be judge and jury in deciding who should keep the toy, suggesting he give the other child a turn in just a little while. Gradually the children will learn that it is much more fun when others share with them, but to make it work it has to be a sharing all around. At game time, children will learn it is not fair to take two turns when some haven't had any. When treats are passed, they will learn to take only their shares and no more, or someone might not have any.

Respecting others. The child who hits, pinches, bites, grabs, or otherwise hurts others, has to be made to realize that he would not like it if someone did that to him. Such a child will gradually learn to use less and less physical violence as he matures socially. The philosophy of the "Golden Rule", (Would you like it if someone did that to you?") will help him grow out of these babyish habits.

Children learn, too, to appreciate the endeavors of their classmates. As they realize that John can make lovely paintings, Jean can sing just like the piano, Sharon is a pretty dancer and Billy can tell stories well, they begin to have an appreciation for the contributions of others.

In community clothing drives, United Fund drives, or Junior Red Cross box-packing, children learn a little about the responsibility for helping others less fortunate. Emphasis should be placed on educating the child concerning the reason for the drive, rather than in encouraging them to bring large amounts of money.

Participating with the group. At the beginning of the term there may be children who prefer to watch during playtime, rhythms, or games before venturing into these activities. Sometimes, taking the child by the hand may be the only push necessary to get him started. Another child might be asked to try to get him to join in, but sometimes, such a child needs more time to observe and to size up the situation. Teachers need to realize this, and not force children the first day, or even the second or third day to enter into activities of which they are afraid. With tact and understanding, the teacher can help children feel secure, and help them eventually to enter into group activities.

What can the teacher do about a child who will not listen to a story, nor join in the singing, nor participate in a game, and spoils such activities for the others? He must do what he can to get this child interested and to cooperate, remembering that as a teacher he has a responsibility to consider the majority of the group. Such a child will have to learn to have respect for others by at least sitting quietly during the story, singing or game time. Eventually, such a child probably will become interested and become a happy participant himself.

Sharing in decisions. Children need to have an opportunity to share in devising certain rules, such as the number of storekeepers that should be allowed in the store at one time, or what to do if they find something that isn't theirs and don't know whose it is. If children are allowed to discuss such problems as they arise, and feel they have had a say in the solution, they will become much more cooperative about observing the rules. Occasionally problems might be solved through a panel discussion. The teacher might ask four or five children to sit at a table to discuss a problem that has come up.

Thinking for himself. Work time provides an excellent opportunity for children to learn to think for themselves, solve problems, be creative and self-reliant, if the teacher provides the opportunity for creative handwork activity, in preference to ones that are always "teacher-directed." For example, instead of directing the children, step by step, how to make a jack-o-lantern out of a cereal box, he might ask, "Can you think how we could make this box into a jack-o-lantern?" The teacher might have in mind that it should be covered with colored paper, with eyes, nose, and mouth pasted on and a string tied through a hole at each side for the handle. The children might have other ideas, however, and the teacher should not belittle their suggestions just because they do not happen to be what he had expected. If he gets no response with his first question, he might have to be more specific. "What could we do, so this won't look like a cereal box?" Someone might answer, "Paint it." This is a worthwhile suggestion and should be appreciated. If someone suggests coloring the box with crayon, the teacher will want to praise him for thinking of another way. Eventually someone will think of covering it with paper. If they are encouraged to think up new ideas, and to test them out as they make their jack-o-lanterns different ways, the experience will be more worthwhile than if all made the same kind.

Social Studies in Kindergarten

Hand in hand with learning to live in the social world, children also learn about their social world. Social studies in kindergarten permeates many activities: singing, rhythms, games, work time, story time, conversation, and playtime. In some form or other, social studies arise quite naturally among five year olds.

Areas of interest. The geographical location from which the kindergarten children come and the background of these children have a bearing on what particular ideas might captivate their interest more than others, but generally the following areas offer possibilities among most children of this age:

The home. (Theirs and those of other peoples in the United States and abroad.)

The neighborhood stores and businesses. (Super markets, bakeries, pet shops, hardware stores, dairies, including where and how they get their products.)

The farm. (Buildings and their uses, animals and what they are used for, people who help the farmer, farm machinery, farm products and what happens to them.)

Transportation. (Trucks, ships, cars, trains, planes, helicopters, including the people who run them and the vocabulary they use.)

Their town. (Theirs and those in other parts of the United States and in other countries. Many will have lived in other communities.)

Community helpers. (Policemen, firemen, doctors, schoolteachers, dentists, gas station attendants, mailmen, milkmen, street repair men, paper boys, safety patrol boys.)

Outer space. (Astronauts, space ships, rockets, planets.)

The school and the public library.

The public zoo and museums.

Stimulating interest. Many times subjects such as those previously mentioned are brought up by the children themselves, in news time or during play. The alert teacher will see the possibilities and want to follow up such leads to develop them into worthwhile learning experiences. Even the beginning teacher, if he keeps these probable areas in mind, can watch for the first show of interest in any one of them and capitalize upon it. He must keep in mind that children will be much more interested in activities which they themselves initiate than those imposed by the teacher. The most successful social studies projects will be those which are of vital interest at the time and close to the lives of the children. Some will be of long duration, others, short. Several might be going on at the same time.

The need for a grocery store might be developed early in the term by children playing in the doll corner, or hinted at by the teacher. Children can plan together how shelves might be made of blocks against the wall, and bring small empty boxes and cans from home to put on the shelves. Such a store would not have to take much space. If located close to a table, children could be taught how to place the table in order for it to be the counter during play time, and how to put it back in place for other activities. Such a project might last the whole kindergarten year. Others might last for only a day, or part of a day.

Not every social studies project or activity will interest everyone. Only a few might be interested in building a boat or train. On the
other hand, others might become interested when it is completed and
many might want to have a ride in it. The teacher might stop the group,
give them some further information so all will have the proper background, and organize the group so that all may have a turn. This is
likely to happen with something such as a train, started by only a few
students. One of them might happen to invite another child to ride on
the train and before you know it, more and more children want to ride,
and the train is not big enough. This is the point at which the teacher
can be a great help. If he calls the group together and helps them develop such ideas as having a ticket seller, conductor, engineer, even a
dining car waiter, and the idea of the train taking only a few at a time,
while others wait in the station, it can become meaningful for everyone
and give all an opportunity to participate. Cardboard tickets will help
make it seem more real and stimulate more enthusiasm, often inspiring
the children to want to repeat it day after day for a while. A circus
might be started and conducted in much the same way.

Whatever is undertaken should be based on ideas that have been
within the experience of most of the group. The teacher need not wait
for an idea to originate from the children, however, but through bulletin
boards, stories, songs, toys and other objects, or even the tickets men
tioned above, can stimulate them to want to start such social studies
activities. Other activity properties which the teacher might provide
are steering wheels, men's white shirts, (to wear while playing doctor
or dentist), fireman's hat, hose for a pump at a gas station, safety boy
belts, and policeman's hat and badge. Even though the teacher has real
ly been the one to "set the stage," so to speak, the children will feel
they have thought of the idea. The good kindergarten teacher will want
to do a certain amount of planning for social studies, in order that this
part of the curriculum is not neglected, but never to the point that it becomes dull and uninteresting.

Unexpected situations involving social studies. Workmen, working in and around the school, can be another source of interest. If the
janitor comes in to fix a burned out bulb, instead of being irritated at
the interruption and losing the attention of the children, the teacher
might better stop the present activity and have the children sit down to
watch him. He can find out what the children know about electricity,
things that run by electricity, how electricity helps us, how it can hurt
us, and encourage them to ask questions about it. In the same way the
teacher can take advantage of the window repair man's visit, or that of
the piano tuner, or an unusual activity which might suddenly start outdoors, in the vicinity of the school, such as the steam roller working in
the street, the building of a new house, or a bulldozer leveling the playground.

Questions which seem simple to adults can stimulate thinking in
the children and make them more aware of their environment and encourage them to observe more thoughtfully.

"Can you think of a question you would like to ask the man about
the steam roller?"

"How does he make it go forward and backward?"

"Why is he running the roller on the new pavement?"

"What is the new pavement made of?"

Even the teacher might not know all the answers, but he need not be afraid to say, "I don't know, but we'll find out."

It should be emphasized that in observing workmen and their machines, extreme care should be taken that the children stay far enough away to be out of any danger.

Taking trips. In some school situations, it is easier than in others to take children on trips to such places as the train station, airport, dairy, pet shop, fire station, zoo, post office, grocery store, bakery, or meat market. In some schools it is very difficult to provide such experiences because of class size, distances involved, or other problems. When trips are taken, they need careful pre-planning on the part of the teacher. Proposed trips should be discussed well in advance with the principal, notes of permission obtained from each parent, and arrangements made, if necessary, for additional help in supervising the children. Children should be well prepared for the trip, know what they are going to see, what they hope to find out, and how they are expected to behave. A "buddy system" will help that none get lost. Mothers or other teachers who assist during the trip should understand clearly what is expected of them. Arrangements for going to the bathroom must be taken into consideration. Even though each child has his own handkerchief, the teacher will find it very handy to have a supply of tissues in case they are needed.

After the trip a simple evaluation might follow, either that day or the next. "Did we find out everything we hoped to find out?" "What did you learn about_____?"

Children might also be asked to draw or paint a picture about something on the trip. A letter of thanks to the place visited might be composed by the group with the teacher jotting down the contribution as quickly as possible as a child thinks of something to say about the trip.

In situations where long trips are limited by number, visits to points of interest in and around the school can provide worthwhile learning experiences. Visits to the school library, lunchroom, office, art, and science rooms can be most informative and interesting to the children. The fire alarm boxes and fire extinguishers in the halls can enrich the study of safety and fire prevention. In the immediate neighborhood of the school, trips can be taken to see fire hydrants, homes and in some locations, traffic lights, mail boxes, gardens, or perhaps stores.

Equally important to having the children go out to get experiences is to bring experiences in to them. This can be done through stamp collections, native costumes worn by the people themselves, and various mechanical contrivances such as clocks and ice cream freezers.

Chapter XIV

Mathematics

Little by little, children become acquainted with numbers, quantities, and mathematical concepts, which form the foundation upon which future mathematical learnings are based. Thus mathematics begins, not in kindergarten, but actually even before that, with their experiences at home. Children entering school vary greatly in their background experience with numbers, but even the most immature child has had some experiences. He knows he is five years old, that he has one sister, or that he wears two shoes. Some children, however, have had much more experience, know the value of money, (that a nickel, a dime and a quarter are worth five, ten, and twenty-five cents respectively), can recognize the numerals on a clock and tell to what numeral the big or little hand is pointing, understand that a dozen means twelve, or can count to twenty and beyond. Whatever has been their experience, children are usually fascinated by numbers and enjoy counting. During the kindergarten year children should have many opportunites for these, and to develop correct concepts of size, quantities, and shapes, all of which will be important later on as they study arithmetic, geometry and other forms of mathematics.

Incidental teaching. Many of the counting experiences in kindergarten will not be definitely planned for, but will come up incidentally, and, because the teacher takes advantage of that psychological moment, it will carry that much more meaning. If a child brings a treat, and the children help the teacher count the children and the cookies, to make sure there are enough to go around, they realize the need and use we have for numbers and counting. "We have thirty-one children and thirty-three cookies. Is that enough for each child to have one?" Although the children do not realize they are doing so, they are beginning the process of division. If the class is having an "apple party" and some have forgotten to bring their apples, the children might watch as the teacher divides some of the large ones in half or into four equal parts in order to make enough to go around, thus developing the concepts of "half," "two halves make a whole," and "whole." Some day there might be a reason to count the number of boys and the number of girls in the group. If the number of children painting each day has to be limited to a certain number, the teacher might count with the children the number of pieces of paint paper that will be needed.

In arranging chairs at the tables, children can learn to put so many on each side. "How many chairs are on that side of the table? How many more does it need?"

In order not to lose knives, forks, and spoons in the doll corner, children might count them at the end of each play time, or, if each has his own box of crayons to use in work time, he might check to make sure all eight colors are there. When children are asked to bring money for charity drives or school projects, the teacher can count the money in front of the children, and explain that five pennies have the same value as a nickle. Many other situations involving counting will arise, but there are other ways the teacher might want to use numbers in her daily routine.

Making "numbers" useful in kindergarten. Most kindergarten rooms have cupboards or shelves which can be numbered. "This belongs in cupboard four." "Please open up cupboard three and bring me a crayon," and other uses of the cupboard numeral will help the child become familiar with them. A bulletin board, with numerals from one to five or ten, might be arranged nearby, showing, for example, one doily for the numeral "1", two shoes for the numeral "2", three clowns for the numeral "3", four clothespins for the numeral "4", and so on. If the child does not know "4", he can count the objects to figure out the numeral.

Putting the same numeral on all the large and small cards belonging to the same lotto game can be a great help to the teacher when they become mixed with another lotto game. If each game has a different numeral, they can easily be straightened out if they become mixed up, and this provides another useful number experience for the children.

Number lotto games can easily be made by the teacher by means of stickers, by placing two birds in one square, three in another, and so on with matching small cards. The backs of puzzle pieces can be numbered, and the corresponding numeral placed in the spot where that particular part belongs. (Children should not rely on the numerals, however, in order to complete the puzzle, but use the numerals only as a last resort if they cannot figure out where the part belongs.)

Not too many kindergarten children are able to grasp the concept of measuring with rulers, but with some explanation from the teacher, the advanced children find a challenge in taking a ruler and measuring the length and width of various articles, such as a block, a piece of paper, or a box. A cardboard ruler might be made of tagboard, and because it will bend, can be used to measure around boxes. With this, a child covering a box with colored paper could measure his own paper and cut it accordingly. In the sand table, the teacher might put large measuring units, such as a pint, quart, cup, half cup, and in their play children will discover for themselves it takes two cups to fill up the pint, and two half cups to fill up the cup. The teacher might demonstrate in front of the group cutting an egg carton in half, thus having two half dozen cartons, and encourage the children to tell the storekeeper whether they want a dozen or half dozen eggs. Actually cutting the dozen carton in half, while the children watch, will help them grasp the concept of a half dozen.

Number experiences in games and songs. Many kindergarten games, described in the chapter on "Game Time in Kindergarten," lend themselves to number experiences without spoiling the fun of the game. In "Old Mother Puss," for instance, the Mother Puss can count her pussies before they hide and then after she finds a few. Such questions as "Have you found them all yet?" "How many more do you still have to find?" help make the child more number conscious, and in this case involves the process of subtraction.

In "Hunting and Finding" games, children count the number of paper objects they find. "Johnny found the most pumpkins." "Which is more, eighteen or thirteen?" Questions such as these help to develop concepts of "more", "fewer", "least", "less", "many", "few", "none", if they do not already understand them. The same is true of "Pumpkin Scramble," in which children scramble to catch the pumpkins as the teacher tosses them into the air.

In "Dog and Bone," the dog has three guesses as to who has taken his bone away. The Children can be taught to keep track of the guesses by saying, "That's one guess." "That's two guesses." "Only one more guess." In "Hot Ball," when several balls are used, the teacher can stop the game every so often by saying "Hold the balls." Then the children can count to see that all the balls are still in the game. In "White Elephant," the child who is choosing the children to be in the middle, does so by bouncing the ball once in front of five children, and as he does so should count, "That's one." "That's two." and so on. In "Ball and Hoop," the children can count the number of balls they get into the hoop, and enjoy keeping score on the blackboard, one scorekeeper can be chosen for the girls and one for the boys. If a girl gets a ball into the hoop, the girls get one point. If a boy does so, the boys get one point. Every so often the teacher might ask for the score. "The boys have five." "The girls have six." She might want to ask the scorekeepers or the whole class to give the score. In "Five Little Chickadees", five children can represent the five chickadees, so that as one at a time flies away the children can see the number that remain. This can also be done with "Ten Little Indians," or children can hold up the correct number of fingers to represent the number of Indians about which they are singing. When Mr. Fox tells what time it is in the game, "Mr. Fox," the children take the number of steps he states as the time, for example, if he says, "One o'clock," all the children take one step, for two o'clock, two steps, and so on. Children who don't already know how to count soon learn in order to keep with the others in the game.

Number fun with the felt board. The felt board with numerals and objects to count has many possibilities. A tree with ten apples can be used as a counting game in this way. The teacher asks the children to close their eyes, then places a certain number of apples on the tree.

"Open your eyes. How many apples are on the tree?" "Can you point to that numeral?"

At first the teacher will want to conduct the game himself to keep it interesting and moving fast, but later he might have a child be the teacher for one turn. The child answering correctly becomes the teacher for the next turn. In this way, the children can play the game by themselves during playtime. The game can be made more difficult by including addition and subtraction.

"How many apples are on the tree?"
"How many have fallen to the ground?"
"How many are there all together?"

For experience with subtraction, the teacher might take some away while the children have their eyes closed and then have them tell how many he has removed. If children use the game during playtime,

the teacher should check occasionally to make sure they have the felt
numerals in correct position, not upside down, nor turned backward.
It might be well to make a small numeral chart on cardboard for them to
use as a guide.

Extending knowledge and concepts. Whenever there is an opportunity to enrich a child's mathematical vocabulary or add to his concepts,
the alert teacher will want to take advantage of it. "Is John's pumpkin
larger or smaller than Billy"s?" "If I cut the apple in half, how many
halves do I have?" "Which block is longer?" are typical questions that
can be asked repeatedly. The names of some shapes can be learned in
kindergarten if they are used in meaningful situations. The "triangle,"
for example, being the name of one of their musical instruments, can be
compared to a triangular block or piece of paper and will be easy for
children to remember. If frequent mention is made of that shape, it will
become a part of their vocabulary.

"Square" and "rectangle" are other shapes they can learn easily.
How to make a "cylinder" and a "cone" can be taught as a technique in
paper sculpture, during the work period. From a flat piece of paper,
children can make a cylinder by rolling the paper and pasting the edges
together in the shape of a roll or cylinder. A cone can be formed by first
cutting out a round circle, then making a cut from the edge of the circle
just to a point in the middle of the circle. When the edges of this cut are
overlapped and pasted together, the result is a cone, which can be used
for the top of a rocket, a hat for a doll, a skirt for a doll, or a wigwam.
Frequent reference to such shapes, in meaningful situations, will help
the child become familiar with them and able to refer to them with ease.

The more meaningful the number experiences, and the more they
are on a level the child can understand, the more he will profit. The
college student, studying the higher forms of mathematics, has built up
his foundation, little by little, in just such a manner.

Building a foundation for the modern mathematics. The School
Mathematics Study Group, frequently referred to as "SMSG", has been
working on a new program of mathematics education, and urges that kindergarten teachers, in addition to providing experiences such as those
mentioned above, try to develop certain fundamental concepts in order
to build a foundation which can be continued in sequential order in the
grades to follow. The teacher himself will need to become familiar with
the following:*

Sets. A set is just another name for a bunch, collection, or group
of things.

Members of a set. The things belonging to this collection. A set
might have only one member, such as the piano in the room or
the teacher's desk.

The empty set. A set might have no members, such as the set of
all the tigers in the room, (if there are no tigers) or trombones
(if there are no trombones.)

A subset. Every member of a subset must be a member of the big
set. The girls of the class would be a subset of the children in
the class.

* School Mathematics Study Group. Mathematics for the Elementary School, Book K, Teachers'
Commentary. Palo Alto, California: Leland Stanford Junior University, 1963. Pp 3-6.

Comparison of sets. We can compare two sets by pairing the members of one set with that of the other, to see if they are equivalent, or if one has more or fewer members than the other. For example:

```
        *           0
        *           0
        *           0
        *
```

(Comparisons might be made between a set of blocks and a set of dolls, or a set of balls and a set of pegs, and so forth.)

Equivalent. When there is one to one relationship, with none left over, we say the sets have been placed in a one-to-one correspondence and the sets are equivalent.

Number. The number of elements of a set is a certain characteristic or property of that set. Other sets, having the same number of elements as that set are equivalent to it. They might not be equal, for example, four dolls are not the same as four blocks, but the number of elements in the set of dolls is equal to the number of elements in the set of blocks.

Greater than. When one set has more members than another, the number of members in that set is greater than the number of members in the other set.

Less than. When one set has fewer members than another, the number of members in that set is less than the number of members in the other set.

More than and fewer than. These expressions are used to describe the members of two sets, while greater than and less than are used to describe the number of members of two sets.

Numerals. The symbols used to represent numbers are called numerals. (They are the symbols 3, 5, 4, etc.)

Joining and removing sets. When one set is combined with a second set, a new set is formed. The new set consists of all the members of the first set plus all the members of the second set, and is called the union of the two sets, (addition). When a subset is removed from a given set, the set left is called the remaining set, (subtraction).

Concerning geometric shapes, circles, triangles, squares and rectangles these concepts are important:

Edge or border. It is the edge or boundary line which determines the shape of a figure. Shapes made of wire, narrow strips of paper, pipe cleaners, pegs, thin sticks can help develop this concept.

Region. Such a boundary, together with its interior, is called a region.

Inside or outside or on. Children can learn the difference in location of a point inside a circle, a point outside that circle and a point on that circle, triangle, or rectangle.

Round or curved. They can learn that a circle is round and that part of a circle is a curved line.

Sides, corners. A triangle has three straight <u>sides</u> and three <u>cor-</u>
<u>ners.</u> A rectangle has four <u>sides</u> and four <u>corners.</u>
<u>Larger</u> than or <u>smaller than.</u> Children can see the difference in
sizes of two circles.
<u>Longer than</u> and <u>shorter than.</u> Children can notice that one side of
a triangle is <u>longer</u> or <u>shorter</u> than another.

The "SMSG Writing Team" in their booklet[*] especially designed
for kindergarten teachers, (based on the information and recommenda-
tions made by a group of kindergarten teachers), suggests ways to introduce this modern mathematics to kindergarten children. A background
for teachers, examples for developing the concepts, and activities and
materials which might be used are given in a clear, well organized manner. It is not intended that a certain period each day be devoted to modern mathematics, but that the teacher will occasionally take the time to
introduce and develop a new concept and to make frequent referrals to it
later on. The teacher must be careful, however, to keep the instruction
informal and appealing. In the SMSG booklet several games and ideas
for use of the flannel board are suggested for group activities, and it is
hoped that the ideas thus developed will be continued informally and incidentally during play, work, and other activities as the occasion arises.
The teacher will need to be alert to spot the children who come from
disadvantaged homes who have had little or no number experience and
will want to give them individual help. If the teacher himself understands the above concepts, and brings them into the picture frequently
in a colorful manner that the children enjoy and understand, he can help
them build strong foundations for modern mathematics. With more and
more emphasis on the importance and value of this new approach to the
teaching of mathematics, the kindergarten teacher will need to familiarize himself as early as possible with effective techniques for including it
in the kindergarten program.

[*]School Mathematics Study Group. Mathematics for the Elementary School, Book K, Teachers'
Commentary. Palo Alto, California: Leland Stanford Junior University. 1963.

Chapter XV

Appraisal of Progress

The needs of a five year old and the ways the kindergarten program is organized to meet them were pointed out in chapter one. In appraising the progress of the children, the teacher might want to refer to their needs occasionally to help him evaluate his part of the kindergarten program.

Self-Evaluation by the Teacher

The kindergarten teacher might ask himself, concerning children's intellectual needs: "Am I actually giving them an opportunity to observe and experiment, or am I always telling them facts, rather than letting them discover and find out for themselves? Am I alert to notice when there is a misconception that needs clarification?" "Do I provide opportunities for all children to express themselves or are some being neglected? Is my speech setting a good example for language development?"

In regard to their social needs: "Do I let children share in making decisions? Have I helped them develop habits of courtesy, or do they interrupt when another child or teacher is talking to me? Have they learned to walk behind, rather than in front of people? Have I succeeded in steering the behavior of aggressive children in the right direction through positive means?"

Concerning their emotional needs: "Does the kindergarten have a happy, pleasant, calm atmosphere? Is there ample opportunity for children to express their feelings as well as ideas in creative work? Do all children feel they "belong?" Do I give deserving praise often? Do I use a positive approach rather than a negative one?"

Regarding their physical needs: "Do I provide large muscle activity, or do I frustrate them by expecting too much in the way of small muscle activity, such as weaving, sewing, or making tiny things? Do I alternate between active and quiet periods or do I let the children become overstimulated? Do I keep in mind their short attention span or do I have them sit for long periods of time? Do they have a chance to move about every fifteen or twenty minutes, or do I expect them to sit too long without changing position? Do I include proper instruction in health, safety, and dental care?"

The kindergarten teacher can improve his teaching through a daily self-evaluation of his work. "It went well today. What made it so?" or "Today wasn't as good a day as yesterday. Why? Children did not follow directions at all. Were all listening when the direction was given, or did I try to talk over voices of children who were talking and not listening? Were the directions too complicated or not clearly given?" or "Children were very disorderly today. Did I supervise as I should have? Was I in a position to see all the children at once or was I occupied with only a few, thus neglecting the majority? Did I try to stop disorder at its onset or did I wait too long? Were there any outside interruptions, beyond my control that upset the class? Have I tried to learn as much as possible about the background of the class?" As the kindergarten teacher learns to evaluate objectively, and realistically, he will profit from his mistakes. Experience will help him to anticipate what children are likely to do, and he will learn to prevent trouble before it starts. The more children with whom he becomes acquainted, the more he will realize that no two are alike, and he will need to evaluate, not only the group as a whole, but the individuals who comprise the group as well.

Appraisal of Progress of Individuals

From the day the child registers for kindergarten, the teacher will start his observation of him. He will probably have time for only a quick glimpse, but through this glimpse may gain valuable insight into a child's background, such as the child's relationship with his mother, his attitude toward other children, or with strangers. The teacher will want to notice any defects such as crossed eyes, speech difficulties, or physical deformities, and will want to obtain as much information as possible from the parent about these matters. It is important to know the occupation of the father, whether or not the mother also works, what supervision there is at home, whether there are other adults who live with the family, the child's playmates, special interests, talents, or hobbies of the child, and any other background information that can be obtained. If it is not possible to discover such information on registration day, the teacher can try to gather it later, in informal conversations with the parent or during a parent conference. As the term progresses the teacher will want to observe the growth of the child physically, emotionally, socially and intellectually. Let us consider how he will do this and what he will want to notice.

How to observe and what to notice. The teacher should know what things he is going to look for, so his observations will be meaningful and not hit and miss. During play time and work time, he will find wonderful opportunities to notice social and emotional growth. Does the child play alone most of the time, or does he play cooperatively with others? Does he share toys with others? Does he respect the rights (and properties) of others? Does he talk over difficulties which arise or does he resort to physical violence? Does he help others who might need help? Is he willing to take turns when necessary? Does he share work materials when asked to do so? Is he happy and comfortable in kindergarten, or is he afraid, withdrawn or worried? Does he cry easily? Is he able to communicate with others adequately?

The child's intellectual growth can be observed in his working with puzzles, lotto and other matching games, building with blocks, and

making things during the work period. Can he find the pictures which
are alike in lotto games? Does he see the places where puzzle parts be
long? Does he solve problems by himself, or does he give up and go to
something else at the first difficulty? Is his attention span unusually
short? Does he remember rules which have been set down? Is he crea
tive? Does he use his imagination?

During quiet activities, such as story time, conversation time,
his ability to listen should be carefully noted. Does he listen to a story
with interest? Is he attentive while others are speaking? Does he follow group directions given by the teacher, or does he have to be told individually before he will act? Children need to develop the ability to
listen, if they are to be successful in reading and academic learning. I
conversation time, can he express ideas well? Can he tell events of a
familiar story in sequence? Can he speak well before the group, or doe
he prefer to remain in the background? Is it a strain upon him to talk i
front of a lot of children? Has his vocabulary increased since he has
been in the kindergarten?

In game time, does he follow the rules of the game and play fair-
ly? During singing time, is he able to sing with the group? Is it an enjoyable experience for him? Is he able to sing alone or with another in
front of the class? During rhythms, is he able to skip and gallop and
execute the other basic rhythms? How is his muscular coordination?

How to make anecdotal records. In keeping records of individual
children, the teacher needs to have some definite system for taking note
and recording information. Notes should be short, but useful, and not
require a lot of time. The teacher will want to take notes as unobtrusive
ly as possible, without letting the children realize what he is doing, perhaps on small pieces of paper, which he will organize later on. In this
form of note taking it is important to record the factual observations,
not interpretations. At a later date the kindergarten teacher or another
person can work from facts but no one can work from interpretations.
If he has a folder or envelope for each child, all notes can be therein,
recording later the important ones on the permanent record. Some
schools provide forms for recording anecdotal notes. Short remarks
and the date are all that are necessary. If there are no such forms,
ruled paper can be used to record the date and a line or two of observations, in chronological order.

At the beginning of the term, the teacher might concentrate on
children who need immediate help and send for the parent as early as
possible. Notes will be of great assistance in such a conference. Following the conference, the teacher will want to record the information
she has obtained from the mother, what took place, and what was agreed
to during the conference. If large envelopes are used, dated samples of
the child's paintings, crayon work, reading readiness test might also be
kept. Some teachers prefer to have a 3 x 5 or 6 x 8 cards for each child,
recording observations periodically on these.

In a class of forty kindergarten children, which is too large but
sometimes exists, it is difficult to do an adequate job of keeping individual records of children. Yet even in a large class, it is important to
know what the children are capable of doing and what growth they are

making. In order to keep aware of the crayon work of each child, once a month the teacher might ask the children to make a crayon picture on 9 x 12 paper about anything they want, and to leave it in school until they are ready to pass into the first grade. The child's name, and the date should appear on each paper. (At the end of the term, the teacher can staple all one child's pictures together and he can make a cover for the collection by folding a piece of 18 x 12 paper in half, and printing on the outside "My Picture Book.") This periodic review gives the teacher an additional chance to notice if a child does not have adequate motor coordination, or if he always draws the same thing. It gives the kindergarten teacher excellent examples, sometimes, of the stages through which children pass in their ability to use crayons, (first, the manipulation and experimentation period, then the "scribbling" period, later the period when "scribbling" takes on meaning and becomes a symbol, and still later the period when the child definitely tries to represent something or creates a well thought out design.) The pictures mean more when the teacher can jot down what the child had in mind, (if anything) but unfortunately, there is not always time to do so. (If anecdotal records are kept, the teacher can record a short remark about the crayon work, including any physical characteristics he might notice, such as squinting, looking too closely at the paper, or using his left hand.)

In addition to a periodic check on the child's crayon ability, the teacher might want to make sure that the child is able to use paste, not only in pasting pictures or making collages, but also in more difficult projects of construction. In large classes, it is sometimes difficult to remember the art activity of each child, when several activities are going on at one time. The "Taking Turn" list, mentioned previously in connection with "Suggestions for Introducing the Work Materials," can be used again in keeping track of the children who have had a turn in a certain experience. On such a list, the children's names are listed vertically, with columns for the various art activities across the top. If a child makes a jack-o-lantern on Monday, the teacher need only to jot down "M" for that child, in the jack-o-lantern column. The same thing might be done at Christmas time if the children make presents, or at Easter if they make hats or baskets. (Some teachers prefer to have all children make the same thing on the same day. If this is the procedure, day after day, the children have little chance to be creative or express their feelings, as they should be able to do in an art period. If done only occasionally, however, it can be a help in checking on the ability of each child.) This too can be referred to in the child's anecdotal record.

An "Inventory of Progress" checklist. Another method of checking on the development of individual children is the use of an "Inventory of Progress" checklist, much like the "Taking Turn" list just mentioned. Down the lift side can be listed the important learning experiences to be considered during the kindergarten year, with the children's names listed across the top. The items of development the teacher selects should be those which are important for this particular group. If in a certain school, every child already knew his colors before starting school, that item would hardly need to be noted, but in a school where children did not learn their colors at home, it would be important to know which ones needed help in that area. The following is an example of a simple inventory.

INVENTORY OF PROGRESS

	Billy A.	John C.	Beth C.	Jane D.	Judy D.	Pat F.	Jay G.	Geo. H.	Iris L.	Sam S.	Joy T.	Bill W.
Is his vision all right?												
Is his hearing all right?												
Does he appear to be in good health? (Properly clothed, fed, cared for?)												
Does he share, take turns, work nicely with the group?												
Does he speak clearly and is he able to express himself?												
Can he take care of his personal needs? (Blowing nose, going to bathroom.)												
Can he tell a simple story?												
Can he say nursery rhymes?												
Does he know how to listen? (To a story, to directions, while others are talking.)												
Can he follow group directions?												
Is he self reliant? (Or does he depend too much on mother, teacher.)												
Does he appear to be happy in school?												
Is he learning to control his emotions?												
Does he have any serious fears?												
Is his attention span normal?												
Does he know colors? (Except:)												
Can he count? (To what number.)												
Does he have proper motor control? (Crayon work, rhythms, work or art media).												

Whatever system the teacher selects should be usable, and not too time consuming, as children are the important factor to be considered, not paper work. However, the notes the teacher takes, and records he keeps will be of great help for planning future kindergarten activities, in parent-teacher conference, in preparing progress reports, and in evaluating whether or not the child is ready for the first grade. Throughout the term, these notes will be helpful to the teacher in his planning as he recognizes the needs of individuals and the group.

How to convey evaluative ideas to parents and first grade teachers. Some school systems send home report cards for kindergarten children just as they do for older children, while others make use of progress reports in which certain descriptions are listed and checked off by the teacher. Still others arrange periodically for parent-teacher conferences.

If there is no specified system, the teacher will want to make use of every possible contact with the parent to help the parent understand how his child is getting along in school. There will be many parents who know little about the kindergarten program, and the teacher will want to be as helpful as possible in giving them an insight into kindergarten life, in order that they understand what the school can do for and expects of the five year old. Perhaps the teacher will want to invite the parents to visit on a specific day, or every so often send home a newsletter, telling what has been going on and informing them of plans for the future. In some schools, a parent-teacher meeting is planned for the purpose of having parents meet the teachers in their respective rooms and to learn about the program. If the teacher has movies or 35 mm. slides, (or even black and white snapshots) of his children engaged in kindergarten activities, he will find them most useful in showing interested parents what happens in kindergarten.

A "Welcome to Kindergarten" booklet, as suggested in the first part of this book or just a mimeographed sheet can be given out to parents the day the child registers for school, and will help to inform them about the kindergarten program, what they, as parents, can do to prepare the child for school, what the school hours are, what scrap items the children might be asked to bring, (such as boxes, ribbon, cards,) suggestions for their children's clothing, (such as having names on clothing, loops on coats so they will stay on the hooks, and mittens fastened to sleeves.) It might also include a word from the nurse, concerning specific things to look for, from a health standpoint, before sending the child to school each day. Parents are usually most cooperative about such suggestions, and especially appreciate learning about the kindergarten program. It is most helpful when the parent has some idea of what takes place in kindergarten before a parent-teacher conference takes place.

As the parent and teacher sit down to discuss the child's progress, the teacher will want to be honest, but, at the same time, realize that Johnny is probably the "apple of his mother's eye," and should approach the interview with this in mind. He will want to emphasize the child's desirable qualities, but, without being critical nor acting as if he "knows it all," also tactfully point out his difficulties and limitations as well.

Not all parents are alike, and the kindergarten teacher will want to proceed slowly in order to feel his way. Some parents have negative attitudes toward schools and the value of education, while others look forward to their children going to school. Some parents have had little or no education beyond grade school, while others are college graduates and expect their children to be also. Some feel economically and socially insecure and feel ill at ease at school affairs. Some have severe means of disciplining their children and if told that the child has misbehaved, might give him a hard beating upon returning home. Some are anxious and over-demanding, with little realization of the standards which are normal for five year olds. They may be pressuring the child to read, with no concept of the reading readiness activities which would be of more value at their child's age level. It is important to try to know how the parents feel and how they might react to the report on their child.

In addition to wanting to know if his child behaves in school, the parent will also be interested in whether or not he will pass to the first grade. The teacher needs to understand what characteristics constitute readiness for learning to read and be able to point these out to parents. A child who cannot follow a group direction, does not listen to stories, has an unusually short attention span, cannot recognize likes and differences, has a limited vocabulary, shows poor motor control, has a short memory, and little control over his emotions probably would meet with failure if he were forced to start reading at this point.

If the teacher feels that a certain child is not ready to start reading instruction, and the parent is reluctant to accept this recommendation, he might have to point out that not every child learns to walk at the same age, nor to talk, and not every child is ready to start reading at the same age. Each child has his own rate of growth. Rather than have him meet with failure, if reading is forced upon him when he is not actually ready, it would be much better for the child to postpone his start in reading until he is ready. He probably will be a much more successful reader later, than if he is forced to start when he is not ready and meets with failure. The teacher will want to explain any tests the child has been given, and their indications, and explain too the importance of the proper attitude, good behavior, and an adequate background of experiences.

Parents will want to know how to help children who are having difficulties and the teacher might suggest reading stories and nursery rhymes, explaining the meanings of words, giving the child as many enriching experiences as possible, pointing out shapes that are the same and different, differences in sizes, differences in sounds and rhyming words. Suggestions might also be made about games they might play on the blackboard or on paper, (such as making three houses alike and one different while the child closes his eyes, and upon opening them, having him point to the one that is different.) If the child is having trouble learning colors or how to count, the teacher might suggest the parent help him at home with the same two or three colors, he is learning at school, until he learns them, before going on to others.

The teacher of kindergarten children has a wonderful opportunity to help parents realize the importance of the school and the home working together, and should do all in his power to create good home-school relations.

The first grade teacher also will appreciate an evaluation of the child's progress in kindergarten. In addition to the child's work samples, tests, anecdotal and other records, he will be interested in learning about the parents, (their attitudes, background, and unusual customs, if any.) Such information can be passed on orally, and should be conveyed in a professional manner and only for the best interest of the child.

Chapter XVI

Services Available

In most large school systems there are many services of which the kindergarten teacher will want to avail himself, in order to make his teaching as rich and as rewarding as possible. In systems where these services are not available locally, the teacher will want to know where he can obtain them, and what he can do on his own initiative.

Services for the Teacher

Audio-visual materials. In a large school system, there is usually an Audio-Visual Department which has available for loan, educational sound films, film strips, slides, and records which the kindergarten teacher may order. Smaller school systems usually borrow their audio-visual materials from county or state centers, and in some cases local colleges. Most of these centers have catalogues available describing materials available.

Each school usually is equipped with the necessary sixteen millimeter movie projector, screen, filmstrip projector, opaque projector, record player, radio and television receivers. The contribution of such audio-visual materials to teaching cannot be overemphasized. Research has shown that learning is more permanent, interest on the part of the pupils is higher, and the experience becomes more real through the use of such materials. If the projectors, record players, radio and television receivers are not available in the school, the teacher might try to borrow them occasionally from friends, parents or business sources. If he himself has a 35 millimeter camera, he can take pictures and have them developed either into transparencies or into filmstrips. Zoo animals, farm animals, community helpers are some possible subjects. There are many excellent audio-visual books, such as Audio-Visual Methods in Teaching by Edgar Dale, and Preparation and Use of Audio-Visual Aids by Kenneth Haas and Harry Packer, which explain the use and how to make transparencies, glass slides, and other aids. Although it is one of the oldest of the visual aids, an opaque projector can be very useful in kindergarten for showing pictures in books, pictures the children have made and birthday, Christmas, Valentine or other cards. It can also be used in preparing bulletin boards. A large piece of white paper is placed on the wall, and the picture, when projected on this paper, can then be traced. Newer developments in the designing and manufacturing of opaque projectors make them a most valuable aid.

Publications. Many large school systems have available publications published by their Board of Education. Many of these can be helpful in other school systems. The Kindergarten Handbook for example, published by the Board of Education in Detroit is a helpful guide for possible activities throughout the year. Publications by the Association for Childhood Education International, and those by the National Education Association are excellent for use in the kindergarten and can be purchased for nominal sums. Every teacher should be on the mailing list of the U. S. Office of Education and the Children's Bureau of our Federal Government in order that they might keep up to date on the latest research, demonstrations and publications. For further information write to the Bureau of Publications, U. S. Government Printing Office, Washington, D. C.

Museum material. Some school systems are fortunate in having a museum or center, which lends out pictures and third dimensional materials (and in some cases even animals) for use in the schools, but if no such service is available, the teacher might want to start his own collection. Pictures can be filed according to the month in which they are likely to be used, if a seasonable item, but if an item such as transportation, health, safety, community helpers, science, or the like, can be filed according to subject. Third dimensional items, such as cardboard jack-o-lanterns, stuffed animals, dolls, and wigwams may be packed in boxes, and labelled for ease in locating. It won't be long before the teacher has his own collection of material, whether or not he can obtain them from a school center, and he will want to have a neat and practical system for caring for them.

Material from industries. Railroads, airlines, supermarkets, dairies, and seed companies represent some of the industries which have pictures or booklets appropriate for kindergarten use. These usually can be obtained without charge. The monthly magazine of the National Education Association and many state association magazines list other free and inexpensive materials in each publication.

Services for Children

The teacher should become acquainted as early as possible with the agencies and facilities in his particular school system which he might use when special help is needed for children with severe problems. If they are not available in his own city or county, they might be available through the county school district, in larger cities nearby, or as services of colleges or universities. The first person to contact regarding special services is the principal. If he is not familiar enough with those that the teacher is interested in, additional information may usually be secured from the superintendent's office in a large city or the county or state department of education if you work in a smaller school system.

The school nurse. Even in large towns, the school nurse is available only occasionally, sometimes only once a week. If a child has a rash or other symptom of disorder, and the nurse is not in the building, he should be referred to the principal or assistant principal, as soon as possible, in case it should be something contagious. The nurse will want to see children who appear to be hard of hearing, to have poor vision, to be undernourished, to have sores which do not heal, or to have any other physical condition which needs attention.

The speech teacher. Serious speech defects should be referred to the speech teacher, if there is one, and if the latter feels the case is severe enough, the child might be included in a special speech class. Often the ordinary activities of the kindergarten program help the child to improve his speech, and it is not necessary to give him special help. If, however, there should be a more serious condition, and there is not a speech teacher, the classroom teacher should refer the case to his principal. Often arrangements can be made with a nearby university or large school system nearby to obtain help, or at least advice.

The "visiting teacher" or "school social worker." Occasionally there is a child in kindergarten who has personality difficulties, behavior problems, or adverse home conditions which require the help of someone with special training, (and time), for dealing with such problems. The teacher should not feel it is a reflection on his ability if he is not able to help such a child, and should not hesitate to refer such a case to the principal. He in turn may arrange for the "visiting teacher" to take over the case. In some parts of the country such specialists are known as "school social workers," rather than "visiting teachers," but basically their work is the same, working with the child, his parents, and the classroom teacher in helping with the child's particular problem.

The Psychological Clinic. In recent years, there has been a marked increase in the psychological services available to children in public schools. Many cities, large and small, now have centers or psychological clinics which offer help, not only through "visiting teachers," or "school social workers" mentioned above, but also through school psychologists and school diagnosticians, who try to diagnose the child's difficulty in behavior or academic work. The kindergarten teacher should refer his cases of such children who seem mentally retarded, who appear subnormal, who have severe behavior problems, or who are socially maladjusted. The principal will know the proper agency or specialist to which to refer the child.

Child Guidance Centers. Throughout the country are scattered some, but not enough, child guidance centers. In Michigan there are a number, the oldest in the nation being located in Detroit. It is under the State Department of Mental Health, and receives its financial support jointly from the state, the county and the city. Others throughout the country are run on a different, but somewhat similar basis. In this type of center, parents and children go once a week for regular appointments where a team of physicians, specializing in psychiatry, clinical psychologists, and psychiatric social workers, help the child with his problems and family relationships. In most cases, a parent must be the one to request this service. The kindergarten teacher should seek the advice of his principal before referring a parent to such a center.

Chapter XVII

Public Relations

Parents are taking a much more active interest in schools today than they did thirty years ago. Since the problems of the teacher shortage, large class loads, and finance have been brought to their attention and since they have been urged to learn more about their schools, more parents are visiting the classroom, attending open houses, participating in parent-teacher groups, and offering their help in solving the schools' problems. Every time the teacher comes in contact with a parent, in any manner whatsoever, he becomes a public relations representative. In business, public relations is a special department, organized for the express purpose of creating good will toward that particular business. In the school system, however, every employee is a public relations person, and should be concerned not only with creating good will toward the school system but in pleasing the public, his employer.

A recent publication by the Board of Education of the City of Detroit, entitled It Takes Teamwork emphasizes this point. In its introduction, Dr. Samuel Brownell, Superintendent of Schools, points out that participation in school affairs between parents and the school staff is a two-way proposition, with school people informing and working with the parents and also parents informing and working with school employees.

The kindergarten teacher will find the "teamwork" idea can become a reality in registration of new children, in parent-teacher meetings and activities, parent-teacher conferences, parent participation in classroom or school activities and in visits to pupils' homes.

In registration of new children. Registration day, as has already been mentioned, provides the first opportunity for the kindergarten teacher to create a favorable impression for the school. A pleasant, polite, and professional attitude is important. Each school has its own system of making the new child and his parent feel welcome. Some arrange for tea or coffee to be served; some plan demonstrations to acquaint parents and children with the kindergarten program; and some arrange for the new children to visit for a half day and actually participate in the class activities. Many of these are difficult to arrange in a large school, however, and in such instances an informative meeting of parents is arranged. In all of these the active members of the local parent group can be of great assistance, as they help with the program, assist the nurse in obtaining information concerning the children's health, and inform the new parents of the parent-teacher activities of the school.

In parent-teacher meetings and activities. The kindergarten teacher might be asked to explain the kindergarten program at a parent-teacher meeting or to a group of parents of kindergarten children. This provides a fine opportunity to inform them that kindergarten is much more than just play, and that kindergarten teachers are far more than baby sitters as many people used to believe. The purpose of the art program may be explained so that parents have a better understanding of the paintings, crayon work, and other products which their children bring home from school. Many parents are not familiar with other im-. portant phases of kindergarten and appreciate hearing about them. This is also an appropriate time to explain the reading readiness program for children who are not quite ready to begin formal reading training after completing a year in the kindergarten.

In addition to participation in parent-teacher meetings, teachers are often asked to help out with school programs, festivals, and other projects of the school, parent group, or community. Some of the jobs are not too pleasant, but cooperation is important and usually appreciated. If the teacher is familiar with the neighborhood and tries to learn more about the community and its particular culture, he will be of more value to the parent group, the children and the school system in general.

In visits to pupils' homes. In some communities teachers are often invited to the homes of pupils for lunch and/or dinner. The opportunity to see first hand the home background of the children can be enlightening in the handling of the children. In the case of death, severe illness or some other tragedy in the home, a short visit by the teacher to the home or hospital is most appreciated. In some school districts kindergarten teachers visit the home of each child once during the first part of the year. These visits should be made by pre-arrangement with the parent in most cases.

In parent-teacher conferences. Many of the conferences which the kindergarten teacher has with parents of his children are informal ones as the mother and teacher chat when the child is brought to school and called for. In such conversations the teacher must avoid discussing other children with a parent or giving out information which should be confidential.

When the teacher finds it necessary to send for a mother to discuss behavior or other problems, he should keep in mind that there is something good to say about every child, in spite of any shortcomings. Parents are often on the defensive, especially if unaccustomed to conferences with teachers. If the teacher begins the interview with a positive approach, is tactful and professional, is a good listener when the parent wants to talk, the interview can be most rewarding. Often the mother is having similar troubles at home, and the very fact that she can talk about the things which are disturbing her, without being pressed or prodded, can help her see things more realistically and improve her own relationship with the child. The teacher should avoid a "know-it-all" attitude, and talk in terms of the parent's feelings. If he has suggestions to offer, he will find them more likely to be accepted if he avoids a dictatorial attitude and leaves himself a way out in case they are not successful. By wording his advice with care and using such expressions as: "Some parents have found this successful---," or "This may not work, but---," or "You may want to try---," he is more likely to gain the cooperation of the parent. *

*California School Supervisors Association. Helen Heffernan, editor. Guiding The Young Child. Boston: D. C. Heath Co., 1959. p. 230.

If a child is having difficulty in school, most parents like to be notified of the trouble as soon as possible. If the teacher intends to have the child remain in kindergarten for an additional term, or placed in reading readiness group instead of the regular class, she should discuss it with the parent as early as possible. Parents want to know how their children are progressing, and in school systems where there are no kindergarten reports, it is up to the teacher to keep parents informed about their children. If a problem arises, it is better to ask the parent to come to the school at some time convenient to her, rather than to put the details in writing. In unusual or severe cases, it is well for the teacher to inform the office and seek the help of the principal or assistant principal in arranging for the interview.

In promoting parent participation. Many parents thoroughly enjoy being asked to enrich the kindergarten program by contributing something in their particular fields, such as demonstrating hobbies, performing with a musical instrument, showing customs of other countries, contributing resource material, or lending collections. Assisting with trips and parties, repairing toys, and promoting safety are other ways in which they might help. Parents who assist in these ways become better acquainted with the teacher, the school, and the problems which they face jointly. In seeking their help, and showing appreciation, the kindergarten teacher can make parents feel a part of the school team, and further develop good public relations.

And So

There are many other kindergarten activities which might be provided, in addition to those mentioned here. Roasting pumpkin seeds, having a vegetable party, a fruit party or a picnic, frosting cookies, having treats, dying eggs for an Easter egg tree, having parties for Halloween, Christmas, and other special days, taking trips, making popcorn, mailing a letter, giving a talent show, or a circus performance, or having a parade are only a few. The teacher will want to be alert to all new ideas and select those which will be most worthwhile for his particular group of children.

Although no formal reading readiness program needs to be carried on in kindergarten, the entire kindergarten program should prepare the child for reading, and of course other subjects as well. Developing language, having many first hand experiences so that reading can be meaningful later, developing concepts, increasing vocabulary, developing the ability to listen, developing a love for books and a desire to learn to read are important phases of the reading readiness program in kindergarten.

The incidental teaching of health, manners, and safety go on continually, but are most effective at those psychological moments when the proper occasions arise.

As the teacher guides his children in these experiences in kindergarten, helping each one to reach his maximal potentialities, and to feel comfortable in his miniature society, he will find a special joy and satisfaction in being a teacher of five year olds, and he for one will realize that the kindergarten year is far more than just "play."

Bibliography

American Educational Research Association. Encyclopedia of Educational Research. Edited by Chester W. Harris. Third Edition. New York: MacMillan Co., 1960.

Anderson, Virgil Antris. Improving the Child's Speech. New York: Oxford University Press, 1953.

Association for Childhood Education International. Reading In the Kindergarten? (1962-63 Membership Service Bulletin.) Washington, D. C.: Association for Childhood Educational International.

Association for Childhood Education International. Science and the Young Child. Washington, D. C.: Association for Childhood Education, 1963.

Backus, Ollie Lucy. Speech in Education. New York: Longmans, Green and Company, 1951.

Barnouw, W. and Swan, A. Adventures With Children In Nursery and Kindergarten. New York: Thomas Y. Crowell Co., 1959.

Baruch, D. W. Parents and Children Go To School. Scott, Foresman and Co., 1939.

Berson, Minnie Perrin. Kindergarten, Your Child's Big Step. New York: E. P. Dutton Co., 1959.

Curtis, Violet H. Our Kindergarten. New York: The Exposition Press, 1964.

Ellis, M. J. Kindergarten Log. Minneapolis: T. S. Denison & Co., 1955.

Forest, Ilse. Early Years at School. First Edition. New York: McGraw-Hill Co., 1949.

Foster, Josephine C., and Headley, Neith Elizabeth. Education In the Kindergarten. Second Edition. New York: American Book Co., 1948.

Foster, Josephine C. Foster and Headley's Education in the Kindergarten. Third Edition, revised by Neith E. Headley. New York: American Book Co., 1959.

Foster, Josephine C., and Mattson, Marion L. Nursery-School Education. New York: Appleton-Century Inc., 1939.

Fuller, Elizabeth Mechem. About the Kindergarten. Washington, D. C.: Department of Classroom Teachers, American Educational Research Association of the National Educational Association, 1961.

Gans, Roma; Stendler, Celia Burns; and Almy, Millie. Teaching Young Children in Nursery School, Kindergarten and the Primary Grades. Yonkers-on-Hudson, New York: New World Book Company, 1952.

Gesell, Arnold, and Ilg, Frances. Child Development. New York:
    Harper and Brothers, 1946.
Gesell, Arnold, and Ilg, Frances. The Child From Five to Ten. New
    York: Harper and Brothers, 1946.
Hammond, Sara Lou and Ruth J.; Dales, Skipper; Sikes, Dora; and
    Witherspoon, Ralph L. Good Schools for Young Children. New
    York: The MacMillan Company, 1963.
Harris, E. K. Responsiveness of Kindergarten Children to the Behav-
    ior of Their Fellows. Washington, D. C.: National Research
    Council, 1948.
Headley, Neith. Foundation Learnings in the Kindergarten. Washingto
    D. C.: National Education Association, Department of Kinder-
    garten-Primary Education, 1958.
Heffernan, Helen, Editor. Guiding the Young Child: Kindergarten to
    Grade Three. Second Edition. D. C. Heath & Company, 1959.
Heffernan, Helen and Todd, Vivian Edmiston. The Kindergarten
    Teacher. Boston: D. C. Heath and Company, 1960.
Hoffman, James and Voris. Kindergarten Creative Units. Minneapolis
    T. S. Denison & Co., 1963.
Huck, Charlotte and Young, Doris A. Children's Literature in the
    Elementary School. New York: Holt, Rinehart and Winston, 196
Hurd, Helen Bartelt. Teaching in the Kindergarten. Second Edition.
    Minneapolis: Burgess Publishing Co., 1959.
Hymes, James L. Jr. A Pound of Prevention. New York: New York
    State Society for Mental Health, 1954, (63 pp.)
Kingsley, W. B. The Kindergarten Way. Philadelphia: Dorrance &
    Co., Inc., 1962.
Lambert, Hazel M. Teaching the Kindergarten Child. New York:
    Harcourt, Brace and World, Inc., 1958.
Lassers, Leon. Eight Keys to Normal Speech and Child Adjustment.
    Speech Aid Series, San Francisco State College. Second Edition
    San Francisco: San Francisco State College, 1949.
Leavitt, Jerome E., Editor. Nursery-Kindergarten Education. New
    York: McGraw-Hill Company, 1958.
Lowenfeld, Viktor. Creative and Mental Growth. Fourth Edition.
    New York: MacMillan and Co., 1964.
Michigan State Department of Mental Health. Child Guidance Clinic
    Program. (Pamphlet.)
Milwaukee Public Schools. Kindergarten Primary Curriculum Guide.
    Milwaukee, Wisconsin: Milwaukee Public Schools, 1960.
Minneapolis Public Schools. An Overview of the Elementary School
    Curriculum. Minneapolis: Minneapolis Public Schools, 1958.
Moore, Elenora Haegele. Fives at School. New York: Putnam, 1959.
Morrison, Ida E. and Perry, Ida F. Kindergarten-Primary Education.
    New York: Ronald Press Company, 1961.
National Education Association, Classroom Teachers Department.
    About the Kindergarten. Washington, D. C.: National Educa-
    tion Association, 1963. (Pamphlet.)

National Education Association, Elementary-Kindergarten-Nursery
Education Department. Teaching Resources for the Kindergarten
Primary Teacher. Washington, D. C.: National Education
Association, 1960.

National Education Association, Kindergarten-Primary Education
Department. Teaching Resources for the Kindergarten Primary
Teacher. Washington, D. C.: National Education Association,
1960.

National Education Association, Elementary-Kindergarten-Nursery
Education Department. Why Kindergarten? Revised Edition.
Washington, D. C.: National Education Association, 1964.
(Pamphlet.)

National Education Association, Research Division. Kindergarten
Practices. Washington, D. C.: National Education Association, 1962.

Northrup, A. H. Child Development Principles In Kindergarten Education. Indianapolis: The Author, 6121 Central, 1954.

Ohio State University Faculty of University School. How Children
Develop. Columbus: Ohio State University, 1946.

Peterson, Helen Thomas. Kindergarten, The Key to Child Growth.
First Edition. New York: Exposition Press, 1958.

Poole, I. "Genetic Development of Articulation of Consonant Sounds
In Speech, " The Elementary English Review, 11, 1934, 159-161.

Portland Public Schools. Kindergarten Curriculum Publication.
Portland, Oregon: Portland Public Schools, 1957.

Read, Katherine Haskill. The Nursery School. Third Edition. Philadelphia: W. B. Saunders Company, 1960.

Rudolph, Marguerita and Cohen, Dorothy H. Kindergarten: A Year of
Learning. New York: Appleton-Century-Crofts Company, 1964.

Sacramento City Unified School District. Key to the Kindergarten.
Sacramento: Sacramento City Unified School District, 1956.

School Mathematics Study Group. Mathematics for the Elementary
School. Book K. Teachers' Commentary, Palo Alto. California: Leland Stanford Junior University, 1963.

Sheehy, Emma D. Children Discover Music and Dance. New York:
A. Henry Holt and Co. Inc. , 1959.

Stendler, Celia B. and Martin, William E. Intergroup Education In
Kindergarten-Primary Grades. New York: MacMillan and Co. ,
1953.

Stone, Dena. Children and Their Teachers. New York: Twayne
Publishers, Inc. , 1957.

U. S. Dept. of Health, Education and Welfare, Office of Education.
What Is a Good Nursery School? Reprint from School Life,
June 1963.

U. S. Dept. of Health, Education and Welfare, Social Security Administration, Children's Bureau. Your Child From One to Six.
Washington, D. C.: U. S. Government Printing Office, 1959.

Van Dyke, P., and Batterberry, H. L. Trails In Kindergarten. New
York: The Exposition Press, 1959.

Van Riper, C. Helping Children Talk Better. Chicago: Science
Research Associates Inc. , 1951.

Watters, L. E. and others. The Magic of Music. Boston: Ginn and
Co. , 1965.

Wills, Clarice Dechent and Stegeman, William H. Living in the Kindergarten. Chicago: Follett Publishing Company, 1950.

Wirick, Martha Moneta. The Kindergarten Year. New York: The
Exposition Press, 1953.

Index

124

Song period, 27
Sound games, 79
Sounds, 56
Speech, classification of, 8
   correction, 8
   development, 6
   disorders, 8
   improvement, 7
   standards, 7
   teaching of, 9
Speech teachers, 113
Sponge painting, 48
Spring, 85-86
Stimulation, 44
Storage, toy, 71-72
Store, children's, 12
Stories, children's, 59
Storytelling, 62-63
Story time, 20, 25
String painting, 47
Student, anecdotal records, 106-107
   appraisal of progress, 105-106
   checklist, 108
   progress checklist, 107-108
Students, home visitations, 115
   observation of, 105-106
   services for, 112-113
   visit to homes, 115
Stutter, 8
Supervision of games, 75

Taking turns, 92-93
Teacher, speech, 113
   storytelling, 62
Teachers, audio-visual materials, 111
   orientation of, 10
   philosophy of, 92
   publications for, 111
   self-evaluation, 104-105

services for, 111-112
Teaching, incidental, 98
   mathematics, 98
   new songs, 52
Techniques, painting, 40
Telephone numbers, 14
Television shows, 67
Thinking, 94
Thought games, 67, 80
Time arrangements of, 25
Timid child, in music, 50
Toilet facilities, 30
Toilets, use of, 17
Tools, digging, 73
Toy storage, 71-72
Toys, 12, 70-72
   wheeled, 73-74
Treats, serving of, 32
Trips, safety of, 97
   social studies, 97

Upset children, 17

Visiting teacher, 113
Visits to pupils' homes, 115
Visual aids, 61-62

Water play, 72-73
Wheeled toys, 73-74
Winter, 84
Wood work, 72-73
Work, 18
Work materials, 38
   introduction of, 40
Work period, 28
   time of, 44
   typical, 43
Wraps, care of, 21

DATE DUE

DATE DUE			
FEB 1 5 1980			
3/3/80			
OCT 1 5 1980			
OCT 2 9 1980			
NOV 1 9 1980			
OCT 5 1981			
OCT 6 1982			
AUG 2 2 1997			